SAVE A FORTUNE ON YOUR HOMEOWNERS PROPERTY TAX!

SAVE A
FORTUNE
ON YOUR
HOMEOWNERS
PROPERTY TAX!

Harry Koenig and Bob Lafay

**Real Estate
Education Company®**
a division of Dearborn Financial Publishing, Inc.

This publication is designed to provide accurate and authoritative information in regard to the subject matter covered. It is sold with the understanding that the publisher is not engaged in rendering legal, accounting, or other professional service. If legal advice or other expert assistance is required, the services of a competent professional person should be sought.

Acquisitions Editor: Jean Iversen
Managing Editor: Jack Kiburz
Project Editor: Trey Thoelcke
Interior Design: Lucy Jenkins
Cover Design: DePinto Studios
Typesetting: Elizabeth Pitts

Published by Real Estate Education Company®,
a division of Dearborn Financial Publishing, Inc.®

Printed in the United States of America

99 00 01 10 9 8 7 6 5 4 3 2 1

Library of Congress Cataloging-in-Publication Data

Koenig, R. Harry.
    Save a fortune on your homeowners property tax! / Harry Koenig and
Bob Lafay.
        p. cm.
    Includes index.
    ISBN 0-7931-2937-0 (pbk.)
    1. Real property tax—Law and legislation—United States—Popular
works.   2. Tax assessment—Law and legislation—United States—
Popular works.   I. Lafay, Bob.   II. Title.
KF6760.Z9K643   1998
343.7305′4–dc21   98-47613
                                                            CIP

Contents

Preface

Most people don't know that it's possible to reduce the property taxes on their personal residence. In fact, not only is it possible, but it is relatively easy, contrary to what you might imagine. It isn't quite as easy as walking into the tax assessor's office, informing him or her that you think your taxes are outrageously high, and expediting a reduction on the spot. But if you're armed with data that properly supports your demand, and you take the proven approach described in this book, you'll have an excellent chance of getting the reduction you deserve. The time you spend gathering the necessary information and preparing your appeal—usually between eight to fifteen hours, depending on your specific situation and knowledge—will be well worth your effort.

Not every homeowner can get a property tax reduction—his or her taxes may not be out of line. But studies have shown that in about 60 percent of America's households there is sufficient evidence to warrant a tax reduction. You could find a number of reasons to justify one. For example, there might be arithmetic errors in your tax records, the age of your residence may be grossly incorrect in the records, you may own a one-story house but be taxed for a two-story house, the dimensions of your land may be wrong in the tax records, or you may not have been given an exemption (as a veteran, for example) to which you are entitled. Most people complain about their federal income taxes, yet few question the property taxes on their residence. That is to say that they don't:

- Analyze their property tax records.
- Look for similar properties sold during the assessment period that could be used to justify a tax reduction.
- Talk to the assessor to request an on-the-spot adjustment.
- Make an effort to prepare an appeal when one is justified.

Among the reasons people don't complain about property taxes is that they don't understand the process. They may think it's not worth the trouble to fight these taxes because they imagine that they can't win anyway. Not true!

According to the International Association of Assessing Officers, an organization dedicated to the proper valuation of property for assessment purposes, more than half of the homeowners who protest their assessments get them reduced.

A study of Rochester, New York, taxpayers by the Lincoln Institute of Land Policy, in Cambridge, Massachusetts points out that only 2 percent of homeowners carried their complaints beyond the local assessor. Of those who did, about half succeeded in winning some relief—an average reduction of 8 percent in assessed value. Those who took their cases to court got an average reduction of 13 percent, and those who went to the Supreme Court got their assessments rolled back an average of 37 percent.

You probably won't need to take your appeal to the Supreme Court of your state, but why shouldn't you be one of those homeowners who have questioned their taxes and won?

This book will help you figure out how to analyze your property tax records and the information used to calculate your tax assessment, how to properly prepare a property tax appeal when the facts warrant it, and how to support your conclusion that a tax reduction is appropriate.

Introduction

A TIMELY MESSAGE TO AMERICA'S HOMEOWNERS

As responsibility for government programs is shifted downward from federal to state to local levels, societal demands do not recede. Effectively, all that changes is who pays to minister to those needs. While this devolution (the passing down through successive stages) is in progress, each lower level of government becomes the court of last resort, and in its new role must find funding to carry out its mission.

Tremendous pressure is exerted to accelerate this devolution process as states start to push unwanted tasks—especially those whose administration carries unknown costs—down to the lowest level of government, that closest to the people—parish, county, city, town, or district. At this level, there are only two choices for funding the operation of government: (1) sales tax and (2) real property tax.

Because sales taxes in most jurisdictions are reaching levels people are unwilling or unable to pay, many communities are relying on real property taxes. Revenues from this source can be raised by increasing the tax rate or by increasing home assessments.

Generally, a combination of the two methods is employed; however, the method of choice is to raise home assessments. By virtue of its abstract nature, most homeowners do not understand how an assessment is determined. Because there are three basic approaches to determining the value of a home (the market approach, the cost approach, and the equity approach used in a few states), there are many opportunities for misinterpretation. Confusion reigns!

The movement to increase homeowners' property taxes is unrelenting. As homeowners, we must do everything possible to ensure our assessments are accurate and that we pay only our fair share.

Save a Fortune on Your Homeowners Property Tax provides a road map to that destination in an easy-to-use tax savings guide for America's homeowners.

The time you invest today will pay dividends—you could save hundreds, perhaps thousands of dollars in the years to come. As much as 60 percent of homeowners pay too much tax!

Save a Fortune on Your Homeowners Property Tax has been designed to help you demystify the tax system by explaining in easy-to-understand terms just how you can determine whether your residence is being fairly taxed. It also provides you with a proven method, *which works in all states*, for gathering and summarizing the necessary data to prepare a successful tax appeal.

From this book you will learn:

- How the property tax system works
- How to determine whether you are being unfairly taxed, and if so, what to do about it
- What to look for to support your case properly
- How to gather and summarize the data needed for a successful tax appeal
- What to say and not say to the tax assessor
- How to file and successfully present your appeal

Forms and checklists, which you may reproduce for personal use, are provided throughout the book. They will simplify your data-gathering efforts and ensure that you don't overlook any important information. The many examples throughout the book help you understand what needs to be done and how to do it.

When you've completed *Save a Fortune on Your Homeowners Property Tax* and properly collected and summarized the data for your appeal, you'll be able to present information effectively to your local tax assessor. If your assessor doesn't agree with your conclusions, you will know how to proceed with an appeal and gather the ammunition you'll need to be successful at the next higher level.

The Eight Steps for Challenging Your Homeowner's Property Tax

Keep in mind that you are appealing the assessed value of your property, not the amount of your property taxes. By lowering your assessed value, the value the government sets on your property, you automatically get a reduction in your property taxes. Your objective is to find a way to lower the assessed value provided by the assessor and to convince the assessor that you are right.

It's very important also to understand why and when to appeal your property's assessed value. For example, if you miss the deadline for filing a property tax appeal, you may have lost your chance until the next year, or you may unnecessarily delay getting a rebate on your taxes. You must understand also the proper reasons for justifying an appeal. If you appeal for the wrong reasons, you will undoubtedly lose your case and will have wasted your time, in addition to looking foolish. So, this book outlines the valid reasons, explains them, and shows you how to organize the facts for a successful appeal.

Let's begin by examining the process for challenging your property taxes. This section provides an overview of the complete process. Once you understand the process, you can more easily learn the step-by-step details that must be accomplished to get your taxes reduced. However, keep in mind that the facts must support any tax appeal you make. It's up to you to decide whether they support your individual situation. This book shows you how to make that decision.

The process has been divided into eight steps:

1. Knowing why and when you should appeal your assessed value
2. Understanding how your property tax is levied
3. Determining the value of your property
4. Adjusting your homeowner's property value
5. Researching your tax appeal
6. Preparing your tax appeal
7. Presenting your tax appeal
8. Enjoying your win

Once you have determined that you should appeal your assessed value, and properly prepared your case, there are several steps in the appeal process that you may have to go through. Don't worry; in most cases you'll never have to appeal higher than two levels of the appeal process; that is, appealing to the staff member in the tax assessor's office and, if denied, presenting your case to the Board of Review. If you have properly prepared, using appropriate supporting data, and properly presented your case to the assessor, you won't have an opportunity to meet the review board—you will have won your case. All of this is explained in the following steps.

STEP 1: KNOWING WHY AND WHEN YOU SHOULD APPEAL YOUR ASSESSED VALUE

The first question that may come to mind is: What is assessed value? It's the value that the assessor determines your property is worth using several valuation methods. These are explained later. However, you should know that the most important one uses the market value, which is based on the prices recently paid for properties similar to yours. The assessor uses information about sold properties, not those listed for sale, to calculate the assessed value of your property. And, as we point out later, a cutoff date is used to select the comparable properties. You won't be using current market data; i.e., data about current sales. Instead, you'll be looking for sales that occurred at or no longer than six months prior to the cutoff date. We'll get into that later also.

You will be appealing your assessed value based on one of the following.

An Assessed Value Too High

Because your property taxes are based on the assessed value of your property, it is important to determine whether this value is fair. The value the tax assessor establishes for your property (the assessed value) is based on its market value or a fraction thereof as determined by the law in your state.

One of the most common and important reasons to appeal your taxes is that the property is overvalued and therefore, overassessed relative to comparable houses in your neighborhood. Comparable houses are ones that are very much like yours in terms of location, style, design, size, and other features. The tax laws are based on an assumption of fair and equal assessments. If your assessment is too high, you are paying more taxes than you should have to.

An Illegal Assessment

One example of an illegal assessment is a property assessed at more than the legal percentage; that is, a percentage of its value arbitrarily set by law. In some states, the assessment is based on a legally established percentage of its market value (or some other similar value).

For example, let's assume that this figure is 50 percent. If the market value of your property is $100,000 and the assessed value is set at $75,000 (75 percent of its market value), you are being overtaxed. It should be assessed at $50,000 (50 percent) in this case.

Sometimes these percentages are applied incorrectly, and if you find that your home is assessed at a higher percentage of its market value than the law allows, you're entitled to have your taxes lowered.

An Unequal Assessment

An unequal assessment occurs when a property is overassessed; i.e., valued at more than its market value. For example, suppose that you recently purchased your home for $100,000, but it is assessed at $130,000. The assessed value, if it is required by law to be set at market value, should be reduced to $100,000.

While an assessment is illegal if it fails to meet the percentage of market value as set by law, an assessment is unequal if it is greater than the market value.

An Error in Your Tax Records

Often you can find errors in your tax records that qualify you for a tax reduction. These may include mathematical errors or errors in recording the details of your house or lot. Two typical errors are found in the age of the building on the property record card or the computation of the building size.

> It's very important to remember that not everyone is entitled to a property tax reduction. It's not automatic and not warranted in all cases. In fact, if you appeal your assessment, be careful that you have supported it with all the appropriate facts. The government can raise your taxes too. A word to the wise: Take your time and gather all the facts before you take any action.

STEP 2: UNDERSTANDING HOW YOUR PROPERTY TAX IS LEVIED

Before you delve into the details of how to prepare a tax appeal, it is important for you to understand how your tax system works and the assumptions behind the property tax system. Later we'll look at a model property tax system to demonstrate how taxes are administered.

STEP 3: DETERMINING THE VALUE OF YOUR PROPERTY

This entails examining your tax records in the local assessor's office to ensure that the data on which your assessment is based are accurate and complete. For example, you'll want to verify that the square footage of your home is accurate in the assessor's records, that the correct style of home is recorded, that the year your home was built is accurate. These factors, if incorrect in the assessor's records, can raise the value of your property. As a result, you pay too much in property taxes.

Determining if your property has been assessed the proper value also involves searching for houses in your neighborhood that are comparable to your property in size, style, construction, and other factors. You may come up with a totally different set of comparables (properties similar to yours that sold during the assessment period) than the assessor. We'll talk more about the type of comparables you need to search for elsewhere in this book.

STEP 4: ADJUSTING YOUR HOMEOWNER'S PROPERTY VALUE

You will fill out some forms to help you evaluate properties comparable to yours using the market data and equity analysis approaches. These approaches to valuing your property will be explained thoroughly in a different section of this book.

You will also be looking for errors on your property record card, and for illegal or unequal assessments, or exemptions which you are entitled to but do not appear in the tax records, such as for veterans or widows. These exceptions are not available in all states, so you must investigate them for yourself.

If you determine that you have a valid basis for a tax appeal, then you will organize your data for that appeal. We'll show you how to do that in a later section of this book.

STEP 5: RESEARCHING YOUR TAX APPEAL

After you have completed the forms needed to determine the value of your property relative to comparable properties, you'll prepare to present this information to your assessor. You will also compile a list of all errors found and indicate why they are incorrect.

In addition, you will make a list of any illegal or unequal assessments or any exemption to which you are entitled but have not received.

At the end of your documentation, you should always calculate and state an amount to which you want your assessed valuation lowered, along with your reasons for choosing that value.

In other words, you want to go to the meeting with your assessor with a figure in mind. It is important for you to present that figure in writing as a conclusion to your documentation. If you don't, the assessor may pick an adjusted value that is unsatisfactory to you.

> ▼ Remember to always calculate and state an amount to which you want your assessed valuation lowered, and your reasons for choosing that value. If you don't, the government representative will select one for you; and it may not be the value you want.

STEP 6: PREPARING YOUR TAX APPEAL

This step will help you decide what information to present to the assessor when all the facts have been gathered; for example, you will want to decide whether or not to complete an equity analysis form. It also will guide you through the preparation process so that you follow the rules and select the right data to present; for example, you'll need to know what a "usable" sale is, which is explained in this chapter.

There also will be tax tips to steer you in the right direction during your preparation. The tax tips are points of emphasis for important items you need to watch out for or rules you need to follow.

A checklist is provided at the end of the chapter so that you don't forget anything in the process. Be sure to check off each item after you have completed it.

STEP 7: PRESENTING YOUR TAX APPEAL

Contact your tax assessor by telephone, arrange an informal meeting, and present your case. Provide the assessor with a copy of your documentation. You'll review it with him or her in an informal, nonthreatening, polite manner. Remember that you are well prepared, and as a result, you will be convincing and persuasive. You will have a good chance to win your case. The assessor will respect you for what you have done because you have presented facts, not simply your opinion that your taxes are too high. Always conclude your meeting by presenting the value you have calculated for the assessed value of your property.

> ▼ Keep in mind the importance of giving the assessor the value you feel your home should be assessed for, based on the facts you have presented.

If the assessor does not agree with your conclusions, your next recourse is to present your case to the tax review board. Or, you may decide to settle for a value slightly higher than your conclusion indicates, but one that the assessor will accept.

Presenting Your Case to the Tax Review Board

The review board may be referred to as the County Board of Taxation, the Board of Equalization, the Board of Tax Adjustment, the County Board of Supervisors, or some similar name. Some of these boards are elected; others are appointed.

The function of the review board is to hear your case objectively and render a decision. Often, but not always, the hearing is conducted in a courtroom. There are legal formalities to follow, but you can find out what these are by attending a review board session or contacting your assessor or the review board administrative office.

Appealing to a Higher Court

There may be a valid reason for you to appeal to a higher court, such as an agency, a specialized tax court, an appeals court, or the Supreme Court in your state. At this point, you would probably want to hire an attorney to represent you. Very few homeowner cases ever reach this level. It is advisable to have a strong case when you go to these levels with your appeal. A competent attorney, who specializes in property tax appeals, or a qualified property tax agent, can help you make this determination. In addition, you should compare the costs and the benefits of appealing higher. Should you win, do the attorney or property tax agent fees leave you with enough of a reduction refund to make it worthwhile?

STEP 8: ENJOYING YOUR WIN!

If you have properly prepared, presented, and won your case, it will be time to celebrate—you will have received a tax reduction. Because your monthly or annual cash outlay for property taxes will have been reduced, you will have extra cash to spend on things more important to you. Just don't forget to invite us to the party.

Knowing Why and When You Should Appeal Your Assessed Value

Now that we've taken a look at the basic process of the property tax system, let's look at the legal basis for appealing your tax bill. We'll begin with an explanation of the publication of the tax rolls.

Once a year, the assessor sets a value on each of the properties in the municipality and issues all the valuations in a complete tax roll that is announced, published, or posted for public review and/or grievance (see Figure 1.1).

During this period of public announcement, the roll is usually considered tentative. This coincides with the grievance or appeal period in most states. After this grievance period, the roll becomes final and is turned over to the tax collector for collection. You should determine when this "tentative assessment" period occurs in your area and consider having an informal discussion with your assessor about your tax bill before this period comes to an end. You can obtain the dates of this period of tentative assessment by calling your local tax assessor's office. In many states, this period occurs toward the end of the year. If you can persuade the assessor to make an adjustment during this period, a change can be more easily made without interference from higher authorities (e.g., supervisor, the county administrator, etc.). At this point, your approach can be informal and won't require a written appeal. Knowing the exact dates of the tentative assessment period also helps you to know how much time you have to gather data and prepare your case.

Every state allows for some kind of local assessment review board. Most states will permit a second party who knows the facts of the case to file a grievance on the owner's behalf. Normally, this would be a tax agent, a tax consultant, or an attorney.

The following is a typical schedule of the major events during a tax year:

Early January	Tax roll becomes final
April or May	Tax rates announced
June to August	Formal appeals accepted
September to October	Review board hearings
November	Results of hearings announced
December	Tentative tax rolls published

NOTE: The above example is not necessarily the schedule in your area. Check with your assessor or county administrator to obtain the exact tax calendar for your state.

In most states a written grievance or complaint is filed in accordance with state law and local regulations. This usually consists of a specific appeal form—perhaps one mandated by the state or one developed locally. The responsibility of finding out what form is needed is up to the filer. Many grievance forms will require the property owner's signature to be witnessed by a notary public.

In most cases, you'll have to pay a nominal fee—usually between $5 and $25—to file an appeal. This fee may not be refundable, even if you win your case or withdraw your appeal.

Filing procedures vary among states. The office of the municipality that made the assessment can tell you how and when to file a grievance. The time period between the opening of the tentative assessment roll and the deadline for filing a grievance is only ten to thirty days in some states. In other states, the period for filing a grievance can be as long as two and a half months, and the publication of the tentative tax roll may be many months earlier. If the deadline is missed for filing a formal grievance, you must wait until the following year to file.

FIGURE 1.1   Sample Tax Roll Homeowner Notification

IMPORTANT NOTICE TO TAXPAYER	**REAL PROPERTY**
OFFICE OF _____ COUNTY ASSESSOR	**NOTICE OF VALUATION**
	THIS IS NOT A TAX BILL

Hearings will begin on the first working day after Notices of adjusted valuation are mailed to taxpayers and continue through _____.

Office Hours: 8:00 A.M. through 4:30 P.M.

Locations: _____

_____

Telephone Number: (___) _____

(___) _____

FAX Number: (___) _____

(___) _____

TAX YEAR	TAX AREA CODE	PARCEL-ID NUMBER	DATE
_____	1155	1973-13-1-20-039	_____

DESCRIPTION OF PROPERTY (May be incomplete)

LOT 6 BLK 31 AURORA HILLS 3RD FLG

13156 E. PACIFIC AVE

ACTUAL VALUATION

TYPE OF PROPERTY	PRIOR YEAR VALUE	CURRENT YEAR VALUE	(+ INCREASE) (–DECREASE)
RESIDENTIAL PROPERTY	190,000	200,000	+10,000

Your last tax bill was $2,015.00*

Your next years tax is estimated to be $2,350.00

This estimate ASSUMES that the mill levy (tax rate) will not change

*Prior years tax does not include fees, interest or special taxes.

An assessment percentage will be applied to the actual value of your property before property taxes are calculated. The assessment percentage for residences is projected to be _____. Generally, all other property, including vacant land, is assessed at ____% A change in the projected residential assessment percentage is NOT grounds for protest or abatement of taxes. The appraisal data used to establish real property value was from the 18-month period ending _____. *If data are insufficient during this time period, Assessors may use data from the five-year period ending _____.

Your property was valued as it existed on January 1 of the current year. The "current year actual value" represents the actual value of your property. The tax notice you receive next January will be based on this value.

Most states have a specific time of the year when an appeal may be filed (e.g., between June 1 and August 15). Likewise, the review board may hear cases only during a specific time of the year (e.g., September through October).

It is recommended that you do not mail your grievance statement due to postal delays and the possibility of it being lost. In some states you don't need to present your statement in advance, but may bring it with you to the review board meeting. In every case, however, make sure you research the tax calendar in your area before you begin.

▼ Some states and/or counties have a formal grievance form that you must complete. Often the form asks you to justify your claim for a lower assessed value by detailing comparable sales data and other related information. Be sure to find out if your taxing municipality requires this form.

There are two types of grievances. One concerns the decision of the assessor regarding an exemption (e.g., a veteran, widow, senior citizen). An appeal or review in this case may not be the same as one concerning the assessment itself. In some states, the taxpayer simply brings the omission of an exemption to the attention of the local assessor and it is corrected. If there is a reason the assessor will not correct it on the spot, an appeal would be necessary.

The second type of grievance concerns the assessment itself and falls into one of these four categories:

1. Illegal assessment
2. Unequal assessment
3. Errors in the assessment
4. Improper valuation of the property

PERSONAL EXEMPTIONS

Exemptions are granted to property-owning individuals for a variety of reasons, which are established by law in each state. If you are entitled to them they are applied against the tax you owe and provide a small tax reduction. For example, in some states, the exemption for a veteran is $50 per year. This isn't substantial, but every bit of tax relief helps.

Typical personal exemptions include:

- Veterans
- Disabled veterans
- Disabled veterans who live in "specially adapted" housing
- Widows of veterans
- Hardship cases (low income)
- Rehabilitated property
- Persons owning mortgaged property
- Fire equipment
- Blind
- Certain agricultural land
- Elderly
- Reforestation
- Property of Red Cross
- Persons 65 years of age and over
- Equipment to prevent air and water pollution
- Tax sale
- Personal property of railroads
- All growing crops (farmland)
- Most tangible personal property, such as furniture, computer equipment, televisions, etc.
- Intangible personal property, such as insurance policies, stocks, bonds, etc.

Note: Not all of these exemptions apply to residential property, and some may not apply in your state. Check with your tax assessor for a list of exemptions that apply in your area.

CHALLENGING YOUR ASSESSMENT

We will now examine in more detail the other reasons to appeal your property tax: illegal or unequal assessments, record errors, and improper property valuation.

Illegal Assessments

An illegal assessment is one that should not have been made or at least, not in the manner in which it was made. Perhaps part of the assessed property is supposed to be excluded from the property tax because it is used by a charitable, religious, benevolent, or nonprofit organization. Or, perhaps part is to be exempt because of its ownership or use. If you are unsure whether an exclusion or exemption applies to you, refer to the tax administration handbook for your state. A copy of this handbook should be available at your tax assessor's office. You can also check with the authorities in your area, such as the tax collector, tax assessor, or county tax administrator.

The following are some forms of illegal assessment to look for.

Property is assessed at more than the legal percentage. For example, the limit is 50 percent of market value and the property is assessed at 75 percent. Contact your tax assessor to find out how properties are valued in your area—at full market value or a legally mandated percentage thereof as determined by your state or local property tax laws.

There is an improper classification of your property. All properties are assessed within a class, such as residential, commercial, industrial, or agricultural. Check to see if your property is properly classified as residential; and if there are subcategories within residential, find out if your property is classified under the right one. For example, there may be ten subcategories for residential housing, where category 9 includes houses that are 2,000 to 2,500 square feet and category 10 includes those larger than 2,000 square feet. Your house may be listed as category 10 when it belongs in category 9. In the tax administration handbook (used by the tax assessor) there may also be pictures of the types of houses that fall in each category. Your house may not even come close to the pictures shown for the category in which you have been assessed. If this is the case, find out if reclassification would lower your taxes.

Assessment is higher than state-issued sales assessment ratio. Sales assessment ratio, calculated by the state tax authorities, is based on the market values within each taxing district, which are announced each year and are available from your local assessor or county tax office. This ratio represents the average at which properties compare to the market value in an area. Sometimes the review board will not change an assessed value if the value you establish does not fall outside a certain percentage of the ratio (e.g., plus or minus 15 percent). On the other hand, the local tax assessor may make the change for you despite the existence of this guideline. Find out from your assessor if this ratio is used in your state, and if so, determine what it is in your tax district. Some states do not use the sales-ratio approach because market values for properties are established each year. In other states, revaluations occur infrequently and sales within the tax year are used to establish average values.

Assessor used the wrong approach in valuing your property according to state manual. For example, the state manual may require the market approach be used to valuate your property, but the assessor used the cost approach. Be aware, however, that under the circumstances involving your property, the cost approach may have been the only approach reasonable or appropriate.

The assessor didn't inspect your property before raising the assessment as required by your state. An inspection may not be indicated on the property record card. If it isn't, ask your assessor if the property was inspected. If you can prove that there was no inspection—which may be difficult—you have a small point to argue. It may be impossible to get a tax reduction based solely on this condition, however, and some states do not require an inspection.

No notice of increased assessment was issued or received. The assessor is required to notify you of an increased assessment by direct mail or public notice. Check to see whether notification was given.

Unequal Assessments

An unequal assessment is one made at a higher proportion of full value than the average of the other parcels on the roll. It can fall into one of three categories.

1. *Property assessed at more than market value.* For example, you can show that the market value of your house is $150,000, but the value set by the tax assessor is $180,000.
2. *Assessments on similar properties are lower.* This demonstrates the equity approach to value. Here, you find comparable properties in your neighborhood that are assessed lower values than your property.
3. *Property recently purchased for less than assessed value.* In this case, the assessed value may be $180,000, but the property, either yours or a comparable one, was sold recently for $160,000.

These categories show the causes of an unequal assessment. You can use the market approach to value, for example, to demonstrate that the value of your property is lower than the value of comparable properties. An approach to value helps you prove your case by comparison, whereas a cause for unequal assessment helps you identify the condition that exists.

An important test of the fairness of your assessment is not just its relationship to market value. It is also whether it is fair in relation to assessments of other properties in your area. For example, if you have land that is worth $8,000 per acre, but is assessed at $6,000 per acre, you may think you are getting off cheaply. However, if nearby land comparable to yours is assessed at only $2,000 per acre, you are paying three times more real estate tax than you should.

Arithmetic Errors

Many times you'll find miscalculations, clerical errors, and other mistakes in the tax records that are used to determine your tax bill. As discussed earlier, you should check for these errors when you inspect your property record card and other records used at the tax assessor's office. Here are some things you can do to check these records.

Check all computations for mistakes, even if you don't agree with or understand some of the cost factors or depreciation percentages. Finding a mistake in a simple computation or a building size—and there seem to be a lot of mistakes—can put you in line for a sizable reduction.

Make sure that you are taxed only for buildings that exist on your property. It is estimated that 5 to 10 percent of all parcels are erroneously inventoried or do not appear on the current assessment rolls at all. Many municipalities have no system to advise assessors of buildings that have been burned, demolished, or otherwise removed. If you are being taxed for a detached garage that no longer exists, you will want to appeal.

Below are some other errors to look for in your records.

The dimensions of your land are wrong. You may own one and a half acres, but are being taxed for two acres, or the dimensions on your record card are incorrect. Your land may measure 100′ by 70′, but the record shows it as 120′ by 70′.

The dimensions of buildings or improvements are wrong. If you own a square building, but the length on one side is listed as being 20 feet and the length of the opposite side is listed as 25 feet, you need to correct the dimensions.

The descriptions of buildings are wrong. For example, perhaps the record shows that your house is constructed of brick, when it has frame construction.

The description of your land is wrong. Perhaps part of your neighbor's land is included on your description and you are being taxed for it.

The wrong property is assessed. The lot and block numbers may be incorrect, or the property you are being taxed on is not yours.

> One of the best sources of data to prove you are entitled to a reduction in your assessed value is to find record or mechanical errors in the tax assessor's records. A word to the wise—look for them.

Failure to note depreciating on-site conditions. Part of your property may be unusable (e.g., it may contain huge gullies), or something on your property may be adversely affecting its value (e.g., quicksand or sulphur odors).

Failure to note depreciating off-site influences. There may be something on the property adjoining yours that materially affects the value of your property, such as a factory producing toxic fumes that drift onto your property.

The grade or quality of improvements are wrong. Maybe you put stones on your driveway, but you are being taxed for a paved driveway.

Important information has been omitted from the record card. For example, the card doesn't show a calculation for depreciation. As a result, your property is overassessed.

The record is out of date. Perhaps your record card hasn't been updated for ten years. There may have been many changes that could lower your assessed value. For example, you haven't maintained your property and it is in poor physical condition, but the records show it is in good condition.

Finished areas are listed incorrectly. Perhaps your record card indicates that your basement is completely paneled and has acoustical ceiling tiles and hardwood floors, when in fact it is unfinished.

Property is assessed in the wrong class. Your residential property may be wrongly classified as commercial.

Property is listed in wrong assessment district. This is rare, but it happens. Perhaps you are being taxed by a district with high taxes, when your property is in fact located in the next tax district where the taxes are much lower.

Personal property is included in your assessment, when it is excluded in your state. Most states do not currently tax personal property, even though they may have many years ago. Some of your personal property, however, may still be shown on the record. If it is, then you are being taxed for it.

Maintenance items are used to increase assessments. Unless there are many items that, when combined, increase the value of your house, your assessment should not be increased for routine maintenance. Look for these on your record card.

Income valuation approach is used in error. State laws usually specify the method to be used to assess properties. See your state manual. Usually, the cost approach is used to value residential properties.

Standard cost manual is improperly used. To check this, you will need access to the cost manual used by assessors in your district. You will have to cross check all the factors selected by the assessor from the manual to arrive at the costs shown on your record card.

Depreciation allowances are made in error. If the depreciation used on your property is significantly different from your comparables, you can challenge it. For example, your house may have been only depreciated 10 percent when the comparables were depreciated 20 percent. Keep in mind, though, that this allowance is based on the condition of your house and of the comparables.

Highest and best use listed incorrectly. You probably won't be able to use this for your residence.

Assessment is higher than construction cost. If you can prove that your recently constructed house cost much less to build than the assessor's cost analysis shows, you can get a tax reduction. This assumes that the assessor used a current, approved cost manual.

Shoddy construction is not noted. For example, you are assessed for average-or-better construction when yours is significantly below standard.

Lack of utilities are not noted. Access to electricity, water, etc., isn't available on your property, but you are being taxed the same as comparable properties that have access to utilities.

Exemptions for property use are not recognized. For example, the property may be used for military purposes; or a portion of the property may be leased to a veterans' organization; or the land has been dedicated to a nonprofit cemetery company; or the property is designated for nonprofit use by a charitable, religious or benevolent organization; or the property is designated as a historic site. These areas of your property should not be included in your assessment.

Owner exemptions are not recognized. The list earlier in this chapter details possible exemptions that you may qualify for. Check with your assessor to verify which ones are used in your area.

Environmental restrictions are not noted. Perhaps part of your property is unusable due to environmental laws or regulations. Make sure these restrictions—which lower the value of your property—are recorded properly on your record card.

Easement restrictions are not considered. Perhaps there is an easement—a written, legal right to use a portion of your property for access to another property—that materially affects the value of your property versus comparable property in your neighborhood. The assessor may not have taken this into account when valuing your property.

The age of the building is listed incorrectly. Perhaps your house was built in 1981, but the tax record shows that it was built in 1996.

> ▼ If the year of construction listed on the property record card for your home is significantly different from the actual year, the assessor will use the wrong comparables in assessing the value of your property. You should be able to get a reduction of your assessed value by demonstrating that the year is incorrect and by supplying the correct comparable sales data.

The number of stories is wrong. For example, the assessor includes a partially finished basement as a story. Verify the square footage listed on your record. Only above-ground square footage counts toward valuing your property. A basement (finished or unfinished) has value, but at a much lower amount per square foot.

The overall description is incorrect. Perhaps your home is described as a three-family dwelling, when actually it is only a two-family building.

VALUATION GUIDELINES

The assessor must follow an official manual. Many assessors are required to follow a valuation manual issued by a state agency, unless they have a valid reason to depart from it. The manuals can be purchased or referenced at a county library. You can buy these manuals at minimal cost, or your assessor may even allow you to examine them while you are in his or her office. However, they can be rather confusing and full of detail and terminology that is not readily understood by the average taxpayer. Not all states have a manual, so don't be concerned if your state does not. In this case, ask your assessor questions about the procedures in your area.

Is it necessary to hire an expert to help you with your case or interpret these manuals? Property owners do challenge assessments successfully without help from experts. However, you may want to consider having a tax attorney or property tax consultant review your documentation before you present your appeal. He or she may be able to point out something that you have overlooked or make suggestions about your materials. The cost should be minimal, and you may feel more confident having had some support or constructive criticism.

After gathering your data, you may also decide to have an expert handle the negotiations with the assessor or review board. There are several advantages to using independent experts. The most important of these is expert knowledge of recent sales, rentals, and market trends, knowledge of the procedures the assessor should be using and knowledge of what the review boards have done in similar cases.

There are various ways in which these consultants may charge you. The consultant may charge by the hour or by the day. In this case, the fee is not contingent upon the outcome of the work. A common arrangement is a flat fee for a preliminary review of an assessment. The specialist reports to the client on the fairness of the assessment and notes any grounds for reduction. If the client is interested in retaining the specialist for further work, the two may agree on an additional fee. In most big cities, there are firms you can retain that will get your real estate taxes reduced for a percentage of the savings. Contingency fee arrangements vary. The principal appeal of this kind of an arrangement is that you pay only for results.

> ▼ A property tax agent or property tax attorney is generally only hired when you are appealling to a review body higher than the board of review, and only then if you think you have a strong case.

There are many ways to handle your appeal. You have to decide how you will be most comfortable and what approach will be most cost effective and successful for you.

REASONS TO CHALLENGE YOUR HOMEOWNER'S PROPERTY TAX

Now that we've reviewed some of the reasons your property may be unfairly taxed, use the checklist below to determine which apply to your assessment. This list will ensure that you don't overlook any area. You can then use this list when you review these errors with the assessor.

Check all that apply to your assessment.

- ☐ Assessed at more than legal percentage
- ☐ Improper classification of property
- ☐ Assessment higher than state-issued sales assessment ratio
- ☐ Assessor used wrong approach in valuation according to state manual
- ☐ Property assessed in wrong class
- ☐ Property listed in wrong assessment district
- ☐ Income valuation used in error
- ☐ Exemptions for property use not recognized
- ☐ Exempt personal property included in homeowner's assessment
- ☐ Personal exemptions not granted or applied
- ☐ No notice of increased assessment was issued or received
- ☐ Maintenance items used to increase assessment
- ☐ Standard cost manual improperly used
- ☐ Wrong property assessed
- ☐ Property assessed at more than market value
- ☐ Assessments on similar properties are lower
- ☐ Property recently purchased for less than assessed value
- ☐ Assessment higher than construction costs
- ☐ Environmental restrictions not considered

☐ Easement restrictions not considered

☐ Property not inspected

☐ Important information omitted from record card

☐ Record is out of date

☐ Mechanical, clerical, computational, or mathematical errors

☐ Depreciation allowances made in error

☐ Failure to note depreciation of on-site conditions

☐ Failure to note depreciation of off-site conditions

☐ Grade and quality of improvements wrong

☐ Shoddy construction not noted

☐ Lack of utilities not noted

☐ Age of home listed incorrectly

☐ Description of land incorrect

☐ Dimensions of land incorrect

☐ Overall description incorrect

☐ Description of buildings incorrect

☐ Dimensions of improvements incorrect

☐ Dimensions of building incorrect

☐ Finished areas are listed incorrectly

Frequently Asked *Q*uestions

Q. How important is it to find out when the assessment period in your state begins and ends?

A. It's vital because if you aren't aware of it, you could lose your property tax appeal because you used comparable sales that occurred in the wrong period. Usually, you can discover the beginning and ending dates by examining your tax bill. They are often shown there. If not, merely call the tax assessor's office and they will inform you.

Q. Should I use comparable sales at the beginning or end of the assessment period?

A. The most effective use of comparable sales is to use those that occurred as close to the ending date of the period as possible, or those within six months of the ending date. These sales normally represent the market values that existed in your marketplace around the cutoff date.

Q. When you believe you are being unfairly taxed, what is the best data to use to prove you are right?

A. The two most effective things to look at are market sales at or within six months of the end of the assessment period, and mathematical or measurement errors. Both can yield substantial tax savings.

Q. What is the significance of discovering that the assessor used the wrong style of house to determine your assessed value?

A. The value per square foot of homes varies considerably by the style of house. For example, people may be willing to pay more for a two-story home than for a ranch-style home. Therefore, if your assessed value is calculated by using the wrong style, you may be overassessed and over-taxed.

Q. What is the most important thing you can do at the end of your property tax appeal presentation?

A. It is vital, at the end of your presentation, to tell the tax assessor what assessed value you believe is correct for your residence based on the facts you presented. If you don't, he or she may try to get you to settle for a value that is unsatisfactory to you. This may occur anyway, but by stating the value you want, the tax assessor is more likely to settle for a value close to the amount you are suggesting.

Understanding How Your Property Tax Is Levied

Before you prepare to make a property tax appeal, it is important that you understand how the property tax system works. You don't need to know every detail about the system, nor how your local government functions, but you should have a general understanding so that you know how your taxes are set, what the monies are used for, and how the taxes are collected.

> ▼ It's not necessary to be an expert in how property taxes are derived, but it is important for you, the taxpayer, to know exactly how the property tax on your personal residence is calculated. You may be paying too much.

Let's take a look at a highly simplified example. Assume that we want to levy taxes in the mythical Village of Taxmania. Let's assume further that there are four properties in the village: two homes, one store, and one church.

To determine how much money they need to raise, the Taxmanian government officials will meet to establish an amount that they think will be sufficient to run their village during the next year. Then, they'll put together a budget for that amount that will pay for the costs of operating each department in their government. In this case, they estimate that they'll need $2,000 generated from real estate (property) taxes.

Their budget outlines how tax monies are to be spent (e.g., schools, any bonded indebtedness the Village has or anticipates, and all other purposes). Then they set about raising the money (the $2,000) through taxation.

First, the Taxmanian tax assessor estimates the full market value of each taxable parcel. (In this example, assume the total appraised value for all taxable parcels adds up to $100,000.)

Next, the assessor converts the appraised values into assessed values. In the state in which Taxmania is located, Taxylmania, the law states that all taxable properties will be assessed at one-half of their appraised value. This is the assessment ratio.

$$\text{(Appraised value)} \times \text{(Assessment ratio)} = \text{(Asessed value)}$$
$$(\$100,000) \quad \times \quad (0.50) \quad = \quad (\$50,000)$$

Then, the Taxmanian clerk (or tax collector) establishes a tax rate that will generate the tax revenues the town needs from the assessed property values.

$$\text{(Tax to be collected)} \div \text{(All assessed values)} = \text{(Tax rate)}$$
$$(\$2,000) \quad \div \quad (\$50,000) \quad = \quad (0.04)$$

Finally, the clerk (or tax collector) prepares and mails the tax bills based on the tax rates and the assessed values for each piece of property. Note that the church property is exempt from property taxes.

	Home #1	Home #2	Store	Church	Totals
Appraised value:	$20,000	$30,000	$50,000	Exempt	$100,000
Assessment ratio:	× 50%	× 50%	× 50%		× 50%
Assessed value:	$10,000	$15,000	$25,000		$ 50,000
Tax rate:	× 0.04	× 0.04	× 0.04		× 0.04
Tax bills:	$ 400	$ 600	$ 1,000		$ 2,000

THE ASSESSMENT PROCESS

In the first part of this example, the tax assessor—or, in some states, an independent appraiser—estimated the value of each taxable parcel. This value varies from one state to another. It is sometimes known as full value, true value, market value, appraisal value, just value, fair cash value, actual value, fair and reasonable market value, or full and fair value in money. Whatever the value is called, it represents, in concept at least, the value of the property in the current marketplace.

All assessments are based on full market value or a percentage thereof. Homeowners in jurisdictions where the assessment is based on full value will find it relatively easy to interpret their tax bills. More than half the states, however, require that local governments base the property tax on some fraction of market value. This can make it more difficult to understand your tax bill. In reading your tax bill, you may feel relieved to discover that the assessment on your $125,000 house is only $80,000. However, if your assessment is calculated at a 50-percent assessment rate, you are actually being taxed as though your home were worth $160,000 ($80,000 divided by 50 percent).

> ▼ In most states, the assessed value of a residence is lower than its market value. This technique often discourages taxpayers from filing an appeal because they think they are getting away with something. The reverse may be true; they may be paying more than their fair share. It pays to find out how your assessed value was determined.

The frequency of appraisals for tax purposes also varies widely from one state to another. Because of the high cost of having appraisals done by independent appraisal firms or by the tax assessor's office staff, a full revaluation of a town, township, community, etc., may not be done every year. In the Village of Taxmania, we assumed that it was done each year.

The appraisal of new construction (versus existing construction), is generally done by the assessor instead of an independent appraisal firm. The assessment of property additions, known as an added assessment, is also done by the assessor.

Looking back again at the first step, the assessor calculated the full value (market value) of all parcels in the Village of Taxmania ($100,000) by adding up the values established for each individual property. He added together the appraised values of the two homes ($20,000 and $30,000 respectively) and the store ($50,000). The church was not included because it is tax-exempt.

ADJUSTING THE ASSESSMENT

In the next step, an assessment ratio was used to adjust the taxable values. Sometimes called the tax multiplier, this ratio will vary widely from state to state. It may be as low as 25 percent, or as high as 100 percent of the market value, or anywhere in between. Often, the adjustment ratio is based on the cumulative value of properties sold during the tax year. It represents the relationship between assessed value and the current market value in the taxing municipality, and is defined by whatever term is used in your state. For example, if properties in the municipality are being assessed at one-half of their market value, the assessment ratio is 50 percent. To put it another way, the properties in the municipality are worth twice as much in the current market as the rate at which they are being assessed.

THE TAX RATE

In the last two steps, the clerk or the tax collector prepared the tax bills and mailed them out. Responsibility for this function will also vary among the states.

The tax rate may be stated as so many dollars per $100 or per $1,000 of assessed value (e.g., $2.05 per $1,000), or as millage—the tax rate expressed in mills, or thousandths of a dollar.

As an additional example of how taxes are computed on a residence, let's use a tax rate of $0.75 per $100 of assessed value, and an assessed value of $50,000. We would calculate the taxes as follows: First, divide the assessed value by 100 to determine the number of $100 units ($50 ÷ 100 = 500). Next, multiply the number of $100 units by the tax rate (500 × $0.75 = $375). The $375 is the tax due that would appear on the homeowner's tax bill.

TAX BILL

Figure 2.1 is a sample tax bill. Let's examine some of the entries.

The top portion of the bill (the part above the phrase THIS IS NOT A TAX BILL—FOR ADVICE ONLY) is a summary of the taxes assessed for the current year. The bottom portion shows the estimated tax for the first and second quarters of the following tax year. These figures are estimated because the tax rate is usually not established until midyear in most states.

Block and Lot Number

These are numbers assigned to uniquely identify the property described in the tax bill. In some communities, the number used may be a permanent index number (PIN), or the property may be identified by address only, or by metes and bounds.

Additional Lot Numbers

Sometimes a property consists of more than one lot. In these cases, the additional lot numbers will be listed. These numbers should be checked by the homeowner to ensure that the correct lots are being taxed.

Rate per $100

The rate is established for use in calculating the amount of tax to be billed for each $100 of assessed value. To determine the amount of tax for any of the categories shown, simply multiply the rate per $100 by the amount of the total assessed valuation divided by $100 (e.g., $181,500 ÷ $100 = 1,815). Multiply 1,815 by any of the figures under "Rate per 100" (e.g., 1815 × 434 = 787.71). The result ($787.71) is shown in the "Amount of tax" column as the amount to be billed for the county tax.

Assessed Valuation—Land

This is the amount established by the tax assessor as the assessed value of the land. This may be set in several ways, such as dollars per acre or part thereof, or by front footage and depth, etc.

Assessed Valuation—Improvements

This is the amount of assessed value for all taxable improvements on the land (e.g., buildings, barns, paved driveways, etc.).

Taxation of Personal Property

Our example does not include the taxation of personal property, such as furniture. In some states, this type of property is included as a separate element of the assessment on your home. Other states tax property located in the home, such as computer equipment, as personal property only when it is used for business in the home. In any event, you should investigate the process in your state, ask questions of the assessor, and be sure that you understand the approach used.

FIGURE 2.1   Sample Tax Bill

1998 FINAL TAX BILL			TOWNSHIP OF ANYTOWN		
Block Number	**Lot Number**	**Qual.**	**Description**	**Rate per $100**	**Amount of Tax**
1	70		County Tax	.434	787.71
			Dist. School Tax	1.077	1954.76
Property location:			Regional School Tax	.763	1384.85
143 Main Street			Local Tax	.476	863.94
Add'l. Lot Numbers			Total Tax	2.750	4991.26
None			Less Deduction		
			for _____	___	___
Account No.			1998-Net Tax		4991.26
Bank Code		400S	Less 1998 Tax		
Mort. Acct. No.			Previously Billed		2486.55
Tax Bill No.			Balance of 1998 Tax		2504.71

1998 – 3rd Qtr. Due Aug. 1, 1998	1998 – 4th Qtr. Due Nov. 1, 1998	Assessed Valuation	
$1252.36	$1252.35	Land	57200
Interest _____	Interest _____	Improvements	124300
Total _____	Total _____	Total	181500

THIS IS NOT A TAX BILL — FOR ADVICE ONLY

1999 PRELIMINARY TAX BILL			TOWNSHIP OF ANYTOWN
Block No.	**Lot No.**	**Qual.**	**Explanation of Tax**
1	70		Preliminary Tax Is Equal To One Half (1/2)
Property Location:			0f 1998 Total Net Tax
Add'l Lot Numbers:			1999-Preliminary Tax Is:
1999 – 1st Qtr. Due Feb. 1, 1999	1999 – 2nd Qtr. Due May 1, 1999		
1247.82	1247.81		2495.63

Frequently Asked *Q*uestions

Q. *What should I do if personal property was included in my assessed value?*

A. Perhaps you should do nothing. That will depend on the law in your state. For example, in some states, personal property is part of the assessed value and, thus, is taxed. In other states, personal property used for business purposes may be taxed also. You must find out the law in your area and proceed from there.

Q. *What is the importance of knowing when property in my area will be revalued for property tax purposes?*

A. When real property is revalued, your assessed value may change, usually increasing, thus raising your taxes. When property is revalued, the tax assessor will have used new sales comparables to derive your assessed value. Therefore, you need to find out what comparables were used and then find others that show your property should be worth less than determined by the tax assessor.

Q. *If the real property in my area is not revalued and my taxes go up anyway, what is the likely cause?*

A. Usually the tax rate is changed more often than properties are revalued. This is caused by the need to raise additional revenues to run the schools and other community operations that receive revenues from the tax base. A new budget is created each year and the expenses of running the government have to be paid from property taxes. Therefore, the tax rate is changed to raise those funds. Usually when this occurs and property is not revalued, there is little you can do to achieve a reduction in your assessed value or your property taxes.

Q. The method for calculating the tax rate varies among different tax areas. Why is that?

A. The calculation of tax rates is created by law in each state. Some states elect to use a tax rate based on so many dollars per $100 of assessed value. Others use a rate per $1,000 of assessed value. Yet others use a millage rate, or a rate based on one one-thousandth of a dollar. The method used is a political issue determined by the taxing jurisdiction, usually the state.

Q. If I live in a state where property is revalued only every ten years, what can I do to get a reduction in my assessed value?

A. The best thing you can do is first examine similar properties in your area, determine the differences, and find out what they are being taxed (or examine their assessed value). If there appears to be inequality, prepare an equity analysis form to use in presenting your case. Also, examine your property record card for any possible errors that affect your assessed value.

Determining the Value
of Your Property

Before you begin analyzing data to determine what value should be set on your property, you need to understand how value is determined and why valuation is important and necessary. Let's examine some of the questions involved.

For any ad valorem tax (a tax law imposed at a rate or percent of a value), it is obviously important to start out with some concept and measure of value. This is because property is to be taxed on the basis of that value.

We might then ask, "How is value to be determined?" Legislatures and courts have shown great creativity in defining a standard for measuring and comparing values among taxable properties in their jurisdictions. They use such terms as cash value, actual cash value, true cash value, fair value, and so forth.

Relatively few states or courts have actually established market value as the ultimate objective to be identified and measured. However, that is what appraisers and assessors, as well as attorneys and even judges, believe is to be measured; primarily, because that is all that can be measured. Without measurability, there can be no basis for comparison, and therefore, no basis for equity. And equity, or "fairness," is one of the ultimate objectives of a property tax system, together with the notion that the value of one's property somehow indicates one's ability to pay taxes.

Therefore, the idea that value is identifiable and measurable has been combined with the search for equity (fairness) in the taxation of property. Thus, the concept of fair market value has emerged as one of the few appropriate methods for establishing taxable value.

THE VALUE OF YOUR PROPERTY

Because an overvalued, overassessed property is one of the most common and most successful grounds for challenging your tax bill, it is extremely important to have a clear understanding of just how valuation works. Establishing the proper value for your property is often the key to your appeal. To win a case like this you must establish that your property's value is lower than the assessed value by one of the four recognized approaches to value:

1. *Market approach.* A comparison of the market value of your house to other houses of equal age, size, location, style, and amenities that sold during the assessment period.
2. *Equity analysis approach.* A comparison of the assessed value of comparable properties.
3. *Cost approach.* An estimate of the cost to acquire an acceptable substitute for a property with like utility.
4. *Income approach.* An estimate of the earning power of a property (not used for non-income producing properties, such as a residence).

For a residential property, you will use the market approach, the cost approach, or the equity analysis approach. Sometimes, you can employ two of these methods together. Generally, the market approach is best because the truest test of value is the price for which a property can be sold in the marketplace. Thus, you should always start by using the market approach. Sales (market) data are available from REALTORS®, appraisers, the tax assessor's office, and companies that specialize in supplying this type of information (e.g., Real Estate Data, Inc.).

In preparing your case, you should do both a market analysis and a cost analysis. The market analysis, however, is far more important, easy to understand, and meaningful. Obtaining cost figures may be more difficult because of the limited sources of information. An appraiser, the tax assessor, and REALTORS® will be the best sources. Sometimes libraries will also carry this information. The cost method is worth pursuing because it is the approach usually used by the tax assessor when compiling the data shown on your property record card.

> ▼ In general, the best approach to value to use when making a property tax appeal is the Market Approach.

Some of the data needed to complete an equity analysis will be relatively easy to obtain. Each property in your tax district will have an assessed value shown in the tax records. These records are available to the public in the assessor's office. However, you will need square footage information for each property to complete this analysis. You may be able to obtain this information from the property record cards, but the assessor may not let you see them. If this is the case, you will have to measure the properties yourself, or search for these measurements in the market data. In addition, the equity approach is not recognized in every state. Contact your assessor to find out if the equity approach can be applied in your area.

Now let's examine each of these methods in more detail.

THE MARKET APPROACH

The market approach, sometimes called the comparative sales approach, is a comparison of the market value of your house to the market value of other homes of equal age, style, size, and location. The market approach is, in general, the best approach to value and the one you should be using for your tax appeal.

Market value is defined as the highest price that a property will bring in a competitive and open market under all conditions requisite to a fair sale, with the buyer and the seller each acting prudently and knowledgeably, and assuming that price is not affected by undue stimuli.

Implicit in this definition is the consummation of a sale as of a specified date and the passing of title from the seller to the buyer under conditions whereby

- buyer and seller are typically motivated.
- both parties are well informed or well advised and each is acting in what he or she considers his or her own best interest.
- a reasonable time is allowed for exposure in the open market.
- payment is made in cash or its equivalent.
- financing, if any, is on terms generally available in the community at the specified date and typical for the property type in its locale.
- the price represents a normal consideration for the property sold unaffected by special financing amounts and/or terms, services, fees, costs, or credits incurred in the transaction.

Think of this approach as an attempt to determine the market value of a property—or the price that it would command in the marketplace—by comparing it to very similar properties. A sample residential market data analysis form is shown in Figure 3.1.

THE EQUITY ANALYSIS APPROACH

The equity analysis approach compares the assessed values of similar properties on a square-footage basis. This approach can be used in the absence of current market data on comparable properties in your area if there have not been any recent sales of homes like yours within a reasonable proximity of your home. You may also use it as an additional example to support your feeling that your assessment is too high.

This method entails making an analysis of comparable homes on a square-footage basis and then making adjustments between the subject property (your home) and the comparable properties. Adjustments are made by comparing items such as materials used in construction, the extras installed in the home, and other features on the property such as a

FIGURE 3.1   Sample Residential Market Data Analysis Form

RESIDENTIAL MARKET DATA ANALYSIS

Subject Property

Legal Description:

PASTE UP PHOTO OF YOUR HOME

Assessor's Property
Identification #:

	Subject	Comp. #1		Comp. #2		Comp. #3	
Property Address							
Distance to Subj.							
Sales Price	$	$		$		$	
Price/Liv. Area S/F	$	$		$		$	
Source of Data							
	Description	**Description**	**Adj. ±**	**Description**	**Adj. ±**	**Description**	**Adj. ±**
Date of Sale and Adjustment/Time							
Living Area S/F							
Location							
Site/View							
Design and Appeal							
Quality/Constr.							
Age							
Condition							
Room Count							
Total							
Bedrooms							
Baths							
Basement							
Finished							
Unfinished							
Garage/Carport							
Porch/Patio							
Other							
Swimming Pool							
Fireplace							
Kitchen Equip.							
Remodeling							
Air-conditioning							
			±		±		±
Net Adj.—Total							
Indicated Value	$	$		$		$	

Comments: _____   Indicated Value by Market Data Analysis _____ $ _____
_____   or $ _____ per S/F

stone driveway. These adjustments are an attempt to allow for differences between the homes—and their assessed values—to make comparisons on a more equal basis. Dollar figures for adjustments may be obtained from valuation companies, state cost manuals, firms that supply cost data (e.g., Marshall & Swift Co.), appraisers, tax assessors, and REALTORS®. When using this approach, all comparables must be within the same taxing municipality as your property because budgets, tax rates, revaluation dates, and assessment ratios vary among taxing jurisdictions. There may be important differences between the way each jurisdiction taxes property that will make comparisons between properties useless. Finally, equity analysis is not an acceptable approach in all states. You should contact your assessor to see if this method is recognized in your state. A sample residential equity analysis form is shown in Figure 3.2.

THE COST APPROACH

The cost approach is used to value residential, industrial, commercial, and special-purpose properties, and will be your best option when no market data are available. This approach is an estimate of the cost to acquire an acceptable substitute for a property with the same utility and similar improvements.

> ▼ Cost data is seldom of much value in a property tax appeal, except in limited situations. Place your emphasis on the market approach.

Standard costs for various construction elements, such as plumbing, electrical, heating, and wall construction are used to cost out the property. *Cost out* means to attach a cost or dollar value to each item for which you are being taxed, such as the cost of the plumbing required for a full bath,

FIGURE 3.2   Sample Residential Equity Analysis Form

RESIDENTIAL EQUITY ANALYSIS

Subject Property

Legal Description:

_____

_____

_____

_____

_____

_____

Assessor's Property
Identification #:

_____

_____

_____

_____

PASTE UP PHOTO OF YOUR HOME

	Subject	Comp. #1	Comp. #2	Comp. #3
Property Address				
Distance to Subj.				
Sales Price	$	$	$	$
Price/Liv. Area S/F	$	$	$	$
Source of Data				
	Description	Description — Adj. ±	Description — Adj. ±	Description — Adj. ±
Date of Sale and Adjustment/Time				
Living Area S/F				
Location				
Site/View				
Design and Appeal				
Quality/Constr.				
Age				
Condition				
Room Count				
Total				
Bedrooms				
Baths				
Basement				
Finished				
Unfinished				
Garage/Carport				
Porch/Patio				
Other				
Swimming Pool				
Fireplace				
Kitchen Equip.				
Remodeling				
Air-conditioning				
		±	±	±
Net Adj.—Total				
Indicated Value	$	$	$	$

Comments: _____

_____

_____

Indicated Value by Equity Analysis $ _____

or $ _____ per S/F

the cost of air-conditioning, the cost of a garage, or the cost of a brick facing on an exterior wall. To use the cost method, you will need current cost figures for your area from a valuation service, such as Marshall & Swift Co., or from your state tax office. Due to the complexity of this method and the potential difficulty of obtaining current cost figures, you may find it extremely hard to use the cost approach for your residence. If you decide to use this method, seek help from an expert. Note, however, that the assessor will use this method to value your property, usually in addition to the market approach.

THE INCOME APPROACH

The last approach to value is known as the income approach. This method won't be helpful to you when you're seeking property tax relief, but it's good to be aware of in case you run across it during your research. Generally, this approach is used for income-producing properties, such as apartments or commercial office buildings. Income-producing property is typically purchased for investment purposes, and from the investor's point of view, earning power is the critical element in defining the property's value.

The income method uses the net income (gross income less operating expenses) derived from lease or rental payments divided by a capitalization rate developed for the type of property and local area in which the property is located. The objective is to determine or estimate the property's value using these factors.

FINAL THOUGHTS

Keep in mind that the best approach to determine the value of your home is the market analysis. The data you'll need to put together a market-based appeal are readily available from many sources. Some suggested sources are REALTORS®, appraisers, tax assessors, and a company called Real Estate Data, Inc. (REDI) headquartered in Florida with representatives throughout the country—see your phone book.

The cost approach is most difficult to compile, and there are limited sources for the cost figures you would need. The tax assessor will generally have valued your property using this approach on the property record card. Don't be intimidated if you are unable to use this approach. Remember that your best approach is the market data analysis. The cost approach can serve as an additional support for your case if you need it.

The equity analysis approach is as easy to use as the market approach, but may not be a recognized method in your state. If it is, however, you'll compile the data using the same comparables you used in the market approach.

Frequently Asked *Q*uestions

Q. What are the most common grounds for preparing a property tax appeal?

A. An overassessed or overvalued property is the most frequent cause that triggers you to prepare a property tax appeal. If you find comparable sales that occurred during the assessment period that were lower in assessed value than your property, you have reason to put together an appeal.

Q. What is the best approach to value to use for a property tax appeal?

A. Usually, but not always, the best approach is the market analysis approach, or the use of sales comparables that are lower in assessed value than your property. Make sure they are within the assessment period before using them.

Q. When is the best time to use the cost approach when presenting my case?

A. The cost approach should seldom be used by the average taxpayer to justify a reduction in assessed value. However, in the absence of market data, you may have to use it. Also, if your residence is on the same site as a commercial property, find an appraiser who is willing to supply you with cost data or help you prepare an appeal using the cost approach.

Q. What should I as the owner do regarding a property tax appeal if I rent my house?

A. We recommend you contact an appraiser or qualified REALTOR® who is knowledgeable about the income approach to value and the rental market. In this case, you will want to obtain information about similar homes in your area that are being rented. You will have to use that data to prove that your home should have a lower assessed value. Your appeal will be based primarily on the property value rental income represents.

Adjusting Your Homeowner's Property Value

When using both the market data analysis and the equity analysis approach to value, it is necessary to make adjustments so the comparable properties and your property can be looked at as equal. You can equalize the properties by compensating for any differences between them. For example, if one of the comparable properties has a fireplace and your property does not, you'll have to adjust the value of the comparable property downward so you can use it as a valid comparison. Or the reverse may exist: if your property has two bathrooms and a comparable property has only one, you'll have to adjust the value of the comparable property upward to use it as a valid comparison to your property.

> ▼ Always apply adjustments for differences between the subject property and its comparables to the comparable property; never make any adjustments to the subject property.

You may want to copy one of the analysis forms shown in Appendix C to record your data and make adjustments to it.

Most adjustments involve physical factors. For examples of some of the more common adjustments, see the list of typical adjustments in Figure 5.4. The dollar figures used are obtained from cost manuals or from data supplied by firms such as Marshall & Swift. An appraiser, the tax assessor, or a REALTOR® can help you obtain the current figures.

The technique of applying adjustments to the comparables changes the value of the comparable property so that when it is compared to your property the result yields a better indication of relative value.

When the comparable property includes an adjustable element that is not shared by the subject property, the value of the comparable is adjusted downward. For example, if the comparable property has a garage and the subject property does not, the overall value of the comparable is adjusted downward by a pre-established amount that represents the value of a garage. The actual dollar amount is determined by periodic studies in similar geographic areas and is published in cost manuals produced by cost valuation firms. When the subject property contains an adjustable element that is not contained in the comparable property, the value of the comparable is adjusted upward.

By adjusting the value of one home by the cost factor of the unshared element, such as the garage, the two properties become more equal in value. The differences between the two properties have been minimized by making the appropriate adjustments to value, treating the element as if it existed on both properties. We assume that the amount of the adjustment is the dollar difference that the presence of the element (in this case, a garage) makes in the selling price or value of a house.

> ▼ The values used for making adjustments vary from one area to the next; sometimes even within the same area. Try to find an appraiser who will help you find the values you need. Appraisers are the best source for this data. The REALTOR® who represented you in the purchase of your home may be able to help you find an appraiser, or assist you in finding data.

Adjustments are typically made to correct differences in time, location, physical condition, and the contributory value of a component.

TIME

Change continually affects the real estate market. During an inflationary period, the value of property tends to rise. In a deflationary period, the reverse is true. The best data for this adjustment are the prices for which properties sold. For example, assume that a property sold three years ago for $150,000 and sold again today for $180,000. That would be an increase of 20 percent over three years or an average for each year of almost 7 percent. An adjustment for time of about 7 percent per year during this period could also be applied to other comparable properties. By way of comparison, a comparable property that sold two years ago would be valued by increasing the prior sales price by 14 percent (7% × 2 years). If it sold for $100,000 two years ago, this time adjustment indicates that the property would be worth about $114,000 today. You must be careful, however, to be sure that no other changes, such as physical improvements, have occurred to the property. If there have been changes, you must also make adjustments for them.

> In recent years, a reasonable adjustment for time differences would be between ¼ to 1 percent per month, depending on the marketplace and inflation.

LOCATION

Where the only significant difference between two properties is location, as reflected by a difference in sales price, an adjustment is made. For example, assume that a property with a better location sold for $120,000, while the property in the poorer location sold for only $100,000. The adjustment for location, assuming all other elements are equal, would be 20 percent ($120,000 ÷ $100,000 = 120%, or a difference of 20 percent). If you were to use these two properties as comparables for your property, and your property has a location similar to the better location, then the value of the poorly located property must be adjusted by adding 20 percent so it can be used as a comparable. If your location was similar to the poorer one, the price of better located property would be decreased by 20 percent.

PHYSICAL CONDITION

Where one property is in good condition and the other needs considerable repairs, an adjustment may be made to compensate for the depreciation or physical deterioration. For example, if two properties in similar locations sold at about the same time, and one was in good physical condition while the other needed considerable repairs, you could use their sales prices to adjust for physical condition. The property in good condition sold for $130,000 and the other sold for $120,000. The difference of 8 percent ($130,000 ÷ $120,000 = 108%, or a difference of 8 percent) can be added to the property in poor condition to compensate for depreciation. The new value of the house in poor condition would be $129,600.

▼ Always consult an appraiser for help in determining this type of adjustment.

FIGURE 4.1   Comparable Sales Data

	Subject	**Comp. #1**	**Comp. #2**	**Comp. #3**
Sales price	—	$140,800	$141,500	$143,000
Date of sale	—	2/99	4/98	6/99
Age	10 yrs.	9 yrs.	9 yrs.	10 yrs.
Condition	Good	Good	Good	Good
Lot size (ft.)	50 × 127	50 × 117	50 × 156	50 × 115
Floor area (sq.ft.)	1923	1962	2008	1936
Full basement	No	800 sq.ft.	1,000 sq. ft.	800 sq. ft.
Garage	2-car	None	None	None
Quality	Good	Good	Good	Good
Location	Good	Good	Good	Good

CONTRIBUTORY VALUE OF A COMPONENT

If there is a difference in the amenities contained in two properties, a dollar adjustment may be made. Items such as garages, fireplaces, and paved driveways fall into this category. Assume that two houses sold at the same time. One that sold for $125,000 had a garage, while the other sold for $119,000 without a garage. The contributory value of the garage then would be $6,000.

To illustrate the application of all these adjustments, let's look at another example. Figure 4.1 shows the adjustable elements to be considered when calculating a final value for the comparable properties and the subject property. Assume the date of valuation is 7/1/99. Figure 4.2 shows the lump sum adjustments made to each property and the concluded value of each property in terms of adjusted sales price.

Adjustments will be required for time, floor area, basement, garage, and lot size.

1. *Time.* Advance in the market of 2 percent per year. No adjustment for sales made within six months of the valuation date. The annual average inflation rate was derived from government agencies or real estate associations.

FIGURE 4.2   Lump-Sum Adjustments and Adjusted Prices for Comparable Rates

	Subject	Comp #1	Comp #2	Comp #3
Time	—	—	+$ 3,400	—
Lot size	—	—	–$ 600	—
Floor area	—	–$ 1,000	–$ 2,100	–$ 300
Basement	—	–$ 20,000	–$ 25,000	–$ 20,000
Garage	—	+$ 7,000	+$ 7,000	+$ 7,000
Total adjustment	—	–$ 14,000	+$ 17,300	–$ 13,300
Actual sale price	—	$————	$————	$————
Total adjustment applied	—	–$ 14,000	–$ 17,300	–$ 13,300
Adjusted sale price	—	$126,800	$124,200	$129,700

2. *Lot size.* Depths of 115 to 130 feet are typical ($600 less for 100 feet of depth and $600 more for 156 feet of depth). Contact an appraiser, tax assessor, or REALTOR® for figures to use for your area.

3. *Floor area.* $25.00 of value per square foot was used. Contact an appraiser, tax assessor, REALTOR® or construction company for average figures in your area.

4. *Basement.* An adjustment of $25 per sq. ft. was used for a full finished basement. The figure used will vary by locality and this one is not necessarily indicative of the adjustment value you should be using for your area. Derived from a cost manual—see an appraiser, tax assessor, or REALTOR®.

5. *Garage.* A value of $3,500 per car from market data was used. Contact an appraiser, tax assessor, or REALTOR® for figures to use.

Note: These values are not necessarily typical, but are shown for illustrative purposes.

Based on the adjusted sale prices in Figure 4.2, the value indicated for the subject property falls between $124,200 to $129,700. Because comparable #3 required the fewest adjustments, it is considered to be the strongest indicator of value. A value for the subject property of $129,700 tends to be substantiated by the data available.

FIGURE 4.3 Home Improvements That May Not Increase Your Assessment

Inside the Home

New furnace	Hot-water heater
Plaster repairs	Painting, wallpapering
Small closets or built-ins	New ceilings
Interior surfacing	Replace wiring
Plumbing fixtures	Light fixtures
New floor surfacing	Leveling a floor
Addition to vents	Remodeling fireplace
New fire exits	New cabinets & countertops
Ventilating fan	New sink
Foundation repairs	

Outside the Home

Repairing masonry	New roof
New porch, steps, stairs	Repair fire escape
New window sashes & sills	Insulation
Weather-stripping	Awnings & window shutters
New gutters & downspouts	Outside painting
Repairing dry rot	Decorative screens
Street trees	Replacing sidewalks
Repairing walks	Replacing sheds & garages
New fences or walls	Addition of retaining wall
Lawns & lawn sprinklers	Replacing garage doors

THE EFFECT OF HOME IMPROVEMENTS ON THE VALUE OF YOUR PROPERTY

The lists in Figure 4.3 show improvements and changes to your property that do not require adjustments and generally do not add to your assessed value (except, as noted, if they contribute to a major improvement in the overall physical condition of the property). The list in Figure

FIGURE 4.4   Elements That Could Affect Your Assessment

Structure (framing and foundation)
Overall quality of the property
Construction (frame, brick, stone, etc.)
Roof (type, slope, presence or absence of gutters/eaves)
Wiring and fixtures (type and grade)
Heating and air-conditioning (type and size)
Detail of finish used in rooms (floors, walkways, trim)
Detail in bathrooms (quantity, type, and grade)
Plumbing (type and grade)
Exterior finish
Windows (storm windows, screens, and type)
Age (the year built, the remaining economic life, effective age)
Square footage

Note: All of these elements must be viewed with respect to their functional utility or usefulness and desirability in the marketplace. Poor design, inadequate lighting, cooling or heating, and rooms that are too small to be functional can have a negative impact.

4.4 shows elements that can affect your assessed value and are considered by the assessor when valuing a property for assessment purposes.

Note: It should be emphasized that a combination of these improvements could result in a considerable increase in the market value of your property. As indicated earlier in this chapter, the physical condition of your property may also require an adjustment.

ADJUSTMENTS FOR LAND VALUE

One of the more significant adjustments is for the value of the land on which improvements (e.g., a house or a building) are located. For example, if one of the comparables you are using sits on five acres of land and your home is on only one acre, an adjustment is necessary to equalize the difference in the amount of land.

Because it is often necessary to analyze differences in size and shape of comparable properties to apply uniform methods of valuation, let's talk a little more about land valuation.

Five Ways to Compare Land Values

When valuating your property, you should follow the method used by the assessor that can be found on the property record card. Similarly, when making adjustments, use the same method selected by the assessor for your property and the comparables.

The five methods of comparing land values are:

1. *Front foot.* This method is based upon the proposition that frontage significantly contributes to value. A front foot is a strip of land one foot wide measured across the front of a property that continues to the rear of the parcel. This distance often is measured in terms of a standard depth and its value is determined using standard-depth tables (found in real estate reference books in libraries or available through appraisers or tax assessors who use this approach). A depth table is a guide used to determine changes in land value caused by variation in lot depth, where land is bought on the basis of a front foot. The front foot method is most often used in valuing commercial and industrial property, but can also be used for residential properties.

2. *Square foot.* This method is used for irregularly shaped land where frontage is not a dominant factor. It is expressed in dollars per square foot. For example, if a parcel contained 10,000 square feet and the value of comparable properties of similar size in your area was $1.00 per square foot, the value of the land would be $10,000.

3. *Acre and section.* An acre contains 43,560 square feet and a section consists of 640 acres. Obviously, this method is used primarily for the valuation of larger properties, such as shopping centers, industrial parks, and ranch and farm properties.

4. *Site.* This method is used when the market does not indicate a significant difference in lot value although there may be a significant difference in lot size. It is used most often in cluster developments, planned unit developments, and industrial sites.

5. *Units buildable.* This method is used for apartment buildings, parking garages, and other properties where the unit of comparison is the selling price per unit. One example would be the number of apartments allowed on a specific site as determined by government engineers or building or planning departments.

Some assessors also employ other arbitrary methods when taxing municipalities where the residences are on one or more acres. They can assign an arbitrary value to the first acre, another to the second acre, and a smaller value to any acreage above that. As long as the method is standard within the municipality and is uniformly applied therein, the tax basis can be considered fair. Market values, however, tend to distort the fairness of methods like this one.

FINAL THOUGHTS

Improper valuation of property, whether it be the land or the improvements, is the key to most tax appeals. You should, therefore, spend as much of your time as possible on gathering data to support the value you establish for your property. It is important that you properly and adequately show its value. Reread this chapter to make sure that you understand valuation.

Frequently Asked *Q*uestions

Q. Is it okay to apply value adjustments for differences between the subject property and the comparables to the subject property?

A. Adjustments are always applied to the sales comparables, not the subject property. The purpose of doing this is to, in effect, make the comparables appear as much like the subject as possible and then to determine an appropriate value for the subject using the adjusted sales prices of the comparable.

Q. *Are the adjustment values for total square footage of a house the same as for a basement?*

A. No. The values used to adjust total square footage, the difference in square footage between the subject and its comparables, is usually higher than the value used for basement square footage. You can see this by examining Figure 5.4, which shows typical adjustments. Consult an appraiser to find out what figures to use in your area.

Q. *What are the most important amenities to make adjustments for?*

A. Differences in the number of car stalls, number of fireplaces, bathrooms, sprinkler systems, air conditioning and decks or patios are the most important ones. See Figure 5.4 for a list of typical adjustments for some possible values to use here. You can also contact an appraiser for help in determining adjustment values.

Q. *What are some of the more important things that affect the assessed value of my home?*

A. The condition of your home is certainly a big factor. Cracks in walls, peeling paint, cracks in the foundation, and conditions of this nature can be used to get a reduction in your assessed value. Look for these and others. See Figure 4.4 for additional ideas.

Q. *Is it okay to use comparables that have considerably different land sizes than my property?*

A. We suggest you find comparables with lot sizes fairly similar to yours, in or near your subdivision. A comparable on several acres a mile or more away from your property probably would not be a good comparable to use if your property is on a city lot which may be only 7,500 square feet. Avoid such comparables.

Researching Your
Tax Appeal

Now we're going to put all the information you've been learning to good use. There's plenty of research for you to do. Remember that you will be searching for data to support a lower assessed value for your property, and that the best way to accomplish that is to gather market data. You'll also be looking for illegal and unequal assessments, and errors in your tax records. Details are important, so take your time and check for all the possible ways to get your assessment reduced.

To properly research your tax appeal, follow the procedures in this chapter.

IDENTIFY COMPARABLE PROPERTIES AND GATHER INFORMATION ABOUT THEM

The first place to begin your research is in your neighborhood. Drive around and look for any properties that are similar to yours in terms of age, size, design, and construction. Note their addresses or relative locations so you can locate them on the tax maps and in the tax records when you visit the tax assessor's office. Later you will also want to determine if they were sold recently, and gather information about the assessments on their land and improvements.

A comparable property is one that is similar in location, age, design, size, and construction to your own residence. A comparable could be a house in your subdivision, built the same year or within a few years of yours, with the same design (e.g., a ranch), the same relative amount of livable area (square footage), and built of the same material such as brick or frame construction. In our imperfect world, however, you may not find such an ideal match, so you will have to compensate for any differences by making adjustments.

A comparable may be identified by locating it physically by its relative location to your residence or other landmarks in the area. It is most important to identify a comparable that is located in the same general area as your own residence; within your subdivision is best. If your home is in an area far away from the comparables you select, your chance of winning your case is minimal.

Likewise, it is important to select a comparable similar in age to your own residence. The depreciation factor of a twenty-five-year-old house will be significantly different from that of a five-year-old house.

The next most important factor is design. Comparing two colonial houses is much more convincing than comparing a colonial to an ultra-modern home. Always select your comparables that have a style similar to your residence, such as a ranch, a two-story or a bi-level, or split level home.

Size differences are less important provided the difference between comparables is not significant. A significant size difference would be 20 percent or more. For example, comparing your 2,000 square foot house to a 3,000 square foot house is a significant difference. Look for a smaller comparable (one with a maximum 10 to 20 percent size difference). You can always compensate for minor differences by comparing the houses on a square-footage basis and then adjusting for the difference in square footage.

Measurements used for a property tax appeal and appraisal purposes are always done on the outside of the house; e.g., the length of all outside walls. This information is used to calculate the total square footage of the living area. Any living area below ground level is not included. There are some areas where below-ground living area is included. Check it out in your area.

Differences in construction materials can also be compensated for. But again, the fewer the differences, the more valid the comparison.

Be sure to identify at least six comparable properties, from which you can select the three that best support your case. Record the information about each comparable on a separate sheet. Blank record forms (Homeowner's Residential Market Data Analysis) have been provided in Figure 5.7 through 5.10 for your use (see Appendix C for additional forms). Later in this chapter, we'll work our way through a few examples to demonstrate how to fill out these forms. As you gather more data about each property, continue to keep all of the information about each property together on the same sheet of paper.

> ▼ Always try to identify six comparables in the beginning, so you can select the three best properties to support your tax appeal.

Once you have identified your comparables, you are ready for a visit to your local assessor's office. Depending on the organization in your state, your property taxes may be administered from a county office or a local office within your municipality. Check the government pages in your phone book for the telephone number and address of the proper office. Call them for information on where your property record card and other related information are located. The object of this initial visit is to familiarize yourself with the information that is available to you, collect data about your comparables, and review your property record card (the assessor's worksheet used to determine the assessed value of your property).

While you are at the assessor's office, you should also examine the tax list and the tax maps. From the tax list you will be able to identify your property and the comparable properties by lot and block number, by street address, or by a permanent index number (if your state uses a parcel identification system to tie together ownership, tax maps, and tax-roll entries).

Before you leave the tax assessor's office, request a copy of your property record card so that you can closely examine it in the privacy of your own home or office. When you go over the record card more thoroughly, look for record errors or anything else upon which you can base your appeal.

IDENTIFY YOUR COMPARABLES ON THE TAX LIST

The tax list is a public record and can be found in the local assessor's office or at the county tax office. It is filed by year and shows all properties within the municipality by owner's name, in alphabetical order, and by lot and block number, in numerical order. You may find books of tax lists for several tax years on display.

Be very careful when comparing the results of your ground search with the tax records. There may be two or more properties that look alike or have the same owner.

Copy all the information about your comparables that you find on the tax list onto a sheet of paper for later use. (You may find it easier to record information directly onto the blank residential market data analysis forms.) This information should include lot and block number, property address, property class, owner's name, the assessed value of the land and improvements, and if given, the size of the land.

LOCATE YOUR COMPARABLES ON THE TAX MAPS

Tax maps for your municipality can be found in the local assessor's office or, for all municipalities in the county, at the county tax office. They may also be accessible in the county clerk's office.

The tax maps will give you the dimensions of your land and the land of your comparables. These maps will also help you properly identify the comparables.

There may be as many as twenty or thirty maps for a larger municipality, and they may be grouped together in several binders. The maps consist of a set of index maps and a set of tax maps (see Figures 5.1 and 5.2). The index maps will help you to identify the specific tax map that contains the particular lot and block for which you are looking. Each index map is a representation of a larger area of the municipality than the tax maps on which the blocks and lot numbers are found. The circled numbers

FIGURE 5.1   Index Map

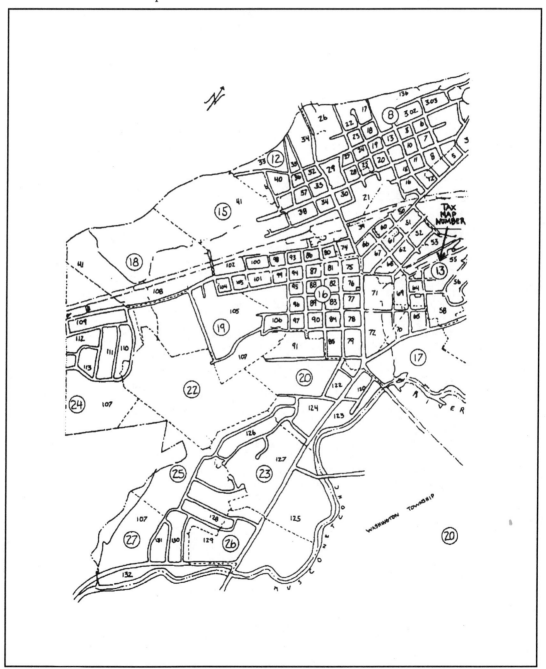

FIGURE 5.2 Tax Map

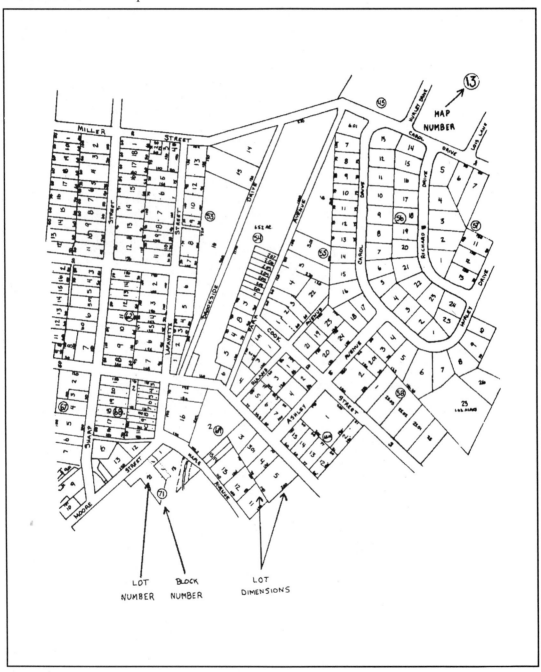

(sometimes enclosed in a square) on the index map refer to the tax map on which the lot and block can be found. The page number on the tax map is usually located in the upper right corner. If the markings are unclear, always ask the office staff for assistance.

When you have positively identified the particular parcel you are looking for on the tax map, record the dimensions and shape of the parcel on a sheet of paper for later use. Never trust the dimensions on a tax map in the assessor's office. Always obtain a map of survey for your property with the exact dimensions. When you purchased your property, one of the many papers you received from your attorney or the title company was a map of survey. It shows the location of your property by use of a ground map. The map of survey will indicate the dimensions of your land, the relative location of any improvements thereon, such as your house, and will indicate the lot and block number or other identification of your property. You should have received a copy of the map of survey with your closing papers. If you don't have one, a copy can be obtained from your closing attorney, or the title or escrow company that handled your closing.

OBTAIN A COPY OF YOUR PROPERTY RECORD CARD FROM THE ASSESSOR'S OFFICE

The property record card contains all the information the assessor used to value your property for tax purposes. It may not be totally accurate, but in some cases, that will be to your advantage. In some states, these cards are not considered public records. Therefore, the assessor is not required to supply you with copies of the cards for the comparable properties that you have identified.

Likewise, in these states, the assessor is not required to furnish you with a copy of your own property record card until a week to ten days prior to your appeal hearing. This means that you will have less time to prepare the information for your appeal.

If you cannot get a copy of your record, you can write down all the information you need onto a sheet of paper. The information you need is the building dimensions, all items being assessed and their assessed values, building age, type of construction, depreciation, land size, any changes in assessed values for any reason, and the computations used for all assessments.

Ask the assessor what method was used to assess the land and note the answer. Compare this method to the method used on your property record card. If the record card shows data for front depth or standard depth, then the front-foot method was used. If square footage is shown, the square foot method probably was used.

Most assessors will furnish the property owner with a copy of his or her property record card upon request. Also ask for the property record cards for the comparables you will be using. If the assessor won't give them to you, ask him or her to give you the total assessed square footage and the year of construction for each of the comparables that you have researched.

He or she may or may not be willing to supply this information. If not, you will have to visit the building department, the engineer's office, or the planning department, where again, you'll have to solicit the cooperation of the staff to obtain the needed information. Usually these offices are located within the same building or in close proximity to the assessor's office. Often, they will bring out architectural drawings and help you secure the information you need from them.

If you cannot acquire the data in any of these offices, you may have to physically measure the comparable houses and/or ask the owners if they can supply the data. This may require a bit of diplomacy, but in most cases you will not have to resort to this kind of research. Figure 5.3 shows a sample property record card.

OBTAIN SALES INFORMATION ABOUT YOUR COMPARABLES

You will also want to review the sales records for properties that have sold in your neighborhood. Check with the tax assessor to determine the cutoff date for comparables for the tax year you are planning to appeal (the

FIGURE 5.3 Property Record Card

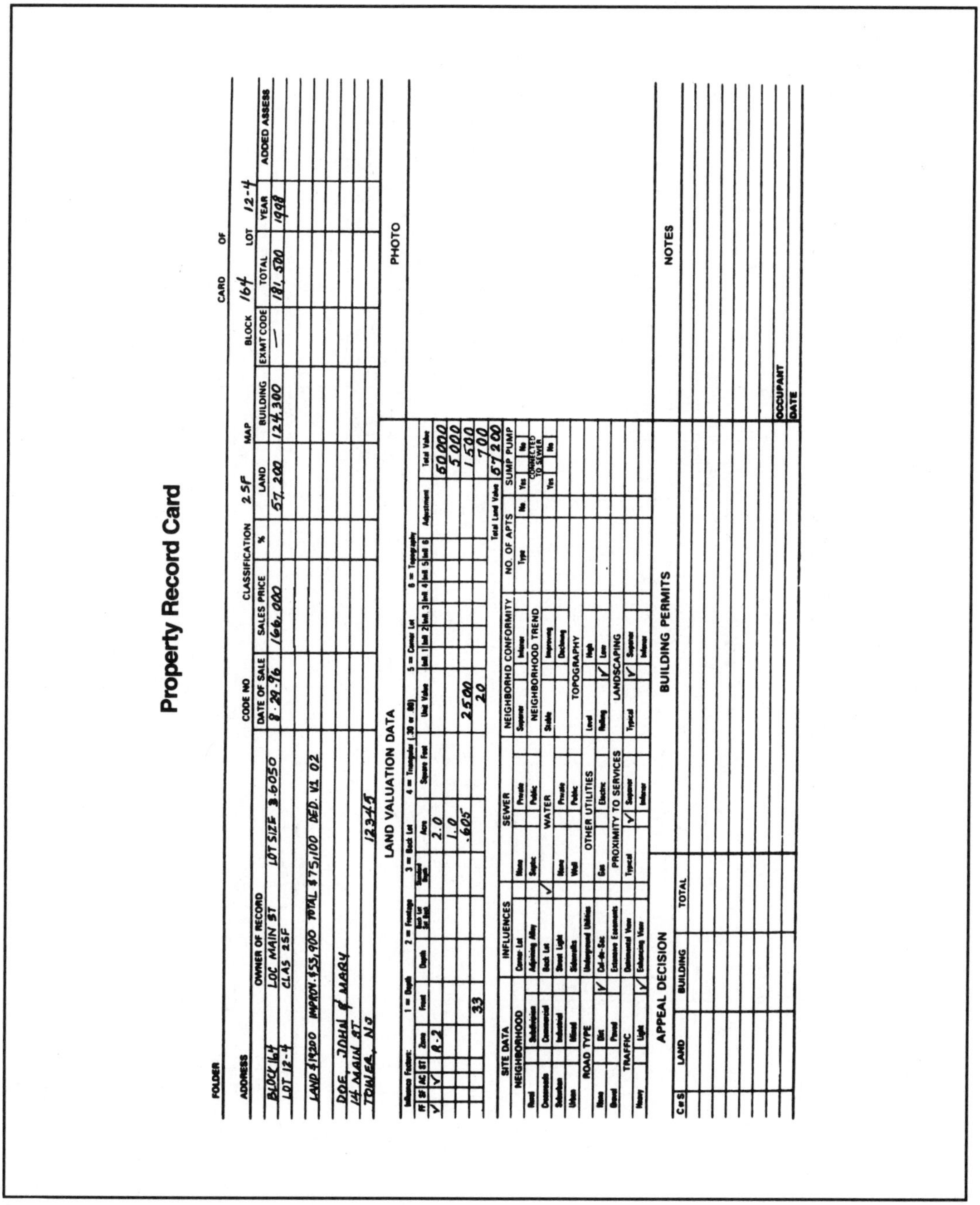

Property Record Card

FOLDER

CARD OF

ADDRESS — CODE NO — CLASSIFICATION 2SF — MAP — BLOCK 164 — LOT 12-4

OWNER OF RECORD	DATE OF SALE	SALES PRICE	%	LAND	BUILDING	EXMT CODE	TOTAL	YEAR	ADDED ASSESS
BLOCK 164 LOC MAIN ST LOT SIZE 3.6050	8-29-96	166,000		57,200	124,300	—	181,500	1998	
LOT 12-4 CLAS 2SF									
LAND $19200 IMPROV. $55,900 TOTAL $75,100 DED. V1 02									
DOE, JOHN & MARY									
14 MAIN ST									
TOWER, NJ 12345									

LAND VALUATION DATA

Influence Factors: 1 = Depth 2 = Frontage 3 = Back Lot 4 = Triangular (.30 or .80) 5 = Corner Lot 6 = Topography

FF	SF	AC	ST	Zone	Front	Depth	Back Lot Set Back	Standard Depth	Acre	Square Feet	Unit Value	Infl 1	Infl 2	Infl 3	Infl 4	Infl 5	Infl 6	Adjustment	Total Value
✓		✓		R-2					2.0										50000
									1.0										5000
									.605		2500								1500
					33						20								700
																		Total Land Value	57200

PHOTO

SITE DATA — NEIGHBORHOOD: Rural, Subdivision, Crossroads, Commercial, Suburban, Industrial, Urban, Mixed

ROAD TYPE: None, Dirt ✓, Gravel, Paved

TRAFFIC: Heavy, Light ✓

INFLUENCES: Corner Lot, Adjoining Alley, Back Lot ✓, Street Light, Sidewalks, Underground Utilities, Cul-de-Sac, Extensive Easements, Detrimental View, Enhancing View

SEWER: None, Private, Septic, Public

WATER: None, Private, Well, Public

OTHER UTILITIES: Gas, Electric

PROXIMITY TO SERVICES: Typical ✓, Superior, Inferior

NEIGHBORHD CONFORMITY: Superior, Inferior

NEIGHBORHOOD TREND: Stable, Improving, Declining

TOPOGRAPHY: Level, High, Rolling ✓, Low

LANDSCAPING: Typical ✓, Superior, Inferior

NO. OF APTS: Type, No

SUMP PUMP: Yes, No

CONNECTED TO SEWER: Yes, No

APPEAL DECISION

C=S	LAND	BUILDING	TOTAL

BUILDING PERMITS

NOTES

OCCUPANT

DATE

FIGURE 5.3   Property Record Card (Continued)

assessment period). For example, if you were appealing taxes for 1999, only comparables prior to June, 1998, may be used. From that date, go back about 6 months. If none are available, use older ones, but adjust for time (e.g., ½ percent per month). Sales records can also be found in the tax office, or they may be centralized at the county level in the county tax office. The sales information is recorded on forms separate from the record cards. The structure and appearance of the form varies from state to state. Ask the office personnel for help. Usually the forms will be grouped by year and by type of property (e.g., commercial, residential, etc.).

Many tax assessor's offices maintain a file of properties that have been sold within their jurisdiction. Others flag sales on the tax maps. Find the information for each of your comparables that indicates the amount and date of the sale. Use only those comparables that have been sold within the allowable period. The more recent the better, but be sure not to use those that are more recent than the tax year cut-off period for which you plan to appeal. Also, if an allowable period is in use (the cutoff date in each state for comparable sales), find comparables during that time frame. That period may be one to one-and-one-half years earlier. Record the data on your form. If there are no sales data available in the tax office, contact a REALTOR® or someone who is a real estate appraiser. Ask him or her to help you gather the information you need.

Another source of sales information is the county clerk's office. There you will find a copy of a deed showing the sales price for each property. To locate the deed, you will need to access the grantee index. This index usually consists of a series of books that are arranged by year with the information listed in alphabetical order by grantee name (the person who bought or now owns the property).

Locate the grantee's name in the index. Opposite his or her name you will find the date that the title was transferred, the deed book number, and page number on which you can locate a copy of the deed. Find the deed book and record the date and sales price on your comparable information sheet. Be sure to also look for any information that indicates that the sale included personal property (such as furniture). If it does, you must exclude that amount from the sales price to make your property comparable. In addition, be sure that the deed matches your comparable (the same lot and block number). Sometimes the grantee will have purchased other properties. You must be positive that you have identified the correct one.

TAKE PICTURES OF YOUR PROPERTY AND THE THREE BEST COMPARABLES

Pictures make your presentation look more professional and thorough. It is a definite plus with benefits that far exceed the inconvenience. Whenever you take a photo of your residence or of a comparable, take it from an angle so both the front and side are visible in the photograph. That enables the viewer to better understand what the house looks like. Remember, a good photo is worth a thousand words, especially if you are trying to show a deteriorated house. Seeing building cracks and peeling paint up close really gets your point across.

PREPARE AN ANALYSIS OF YOUR TAX CHALLENGE RESEARCH

Remember that there are four main reasons to challenge your property tax: (1) misvalued property, (2) an illegal assessment, (3) an unequal assessment, and (4) record errors. Carefully analyze the information you've collected and search for errors in each of these areas. First, look at the information you've collected about your property and your comparables to see if you can make a case that your home is overassessed compared to similar properties.

Select the three comparables that best support your case (those that have a lower tax and assessed value) and record all information on a blank analysis record form (found in Figures 5.7 through 5.10). Use the guidelines in Figure 5.5 and the example in Figure 5.6 to help you record the proper data.

Residential Market Data Analysis Approach

This approach consists of obtaining information on the sales of three similar homes located as close to your property as possible. The sales prices of these homes are then adjusted to determine a fair market value for your property.

The information you should gather to complete this analysis includes:

1. Location
2. Style (two-story, ranch, split-level, colonial, etc.; the style should be similar to the subject's)
3. Basement (finished or unfinished)
4. Size (square footage of living area should be as close in size to your home as possible); only living area above ground level is counted.
5. Number of bedrooms
6. Number of bathrooms
7. Central air conditioning
8. Fireplaces
9. Garage capacity (one, two, or more cars)

Enter all appropriate data on the blank Residential Market Data Analysis record forms provided.

For items 1 and 2, it is important that the comparables are as similar to your home as possible. A dollar adjustment for these elements is difficult to prove.

Each of the items from 6 through 9 has a value in the marketplace. You will assign a value and make adjustments for each one relative to your property. Area REALTORS® and local appraisers will be able to supply you with standard value ranges for these adjustments because they use the values for acquiring bank loans and making appraisals. Figure 5.4 illustrates typical adjustment values. Keep in mind that the adjustment values shown are not necessarily representative of the values you can use in your area of the country.

FIGURE 5.4 Typical Adjustments for Residential Properties

Type	Homes Valued At		
	$75–$100,000	$100–$175,000	$175–$250,000
Bedroom	$1,000	$1,500	$2,000
Baths:			
Full	$2,500	$2,500	$2,500
¾	$2,000	$2,000	$2,000
½	$1,500	$1,500	$1,500
¼	$1,000	$1,000	$1,000
Air conditioning	$1,500	$2,000	$2,500
Evap. cooling	$1,000	$1,000	$1,000
Attic fan	$ 500	$ 500	$ 500
Garage	$2,000/Stall	$3,000/Stall	$4,000/Stall
Carport	$1,000/Stall	$1,500/Stall	$2,000/Stall
Fireplace	$1,500	$1,500	$1,500
Sprinkler system	$1,500	$1,500	$1,500
Hot tub	$ 500	$ 500	$ 500
Deck	$ 500–$1,000	$1,000–$2,000	$2,000–$3,000
Covered patio	$ 500–$1,000	$1,000–$1,500	$1,500–$2,000
Encl. Porch/Sun Rm.	$2,000	$3,000	$4,000–$5,000
Basement:			
Finished			
Regular	$15–$16/Sq.Ft.	$17–$18/Sq.Ft.	$19–$20/Sq.Ft.
Walkout	$20–$21/Sq.Ft.	$22–$23/Sq.Ft.	$24–$25/Sq.Ft.
Unfinished			
Regular	$10–$11/Sq.Ft.	$12–$13/Sq.Ft.	$14–$15/Sq.Ft.
Walkout	$18/Sq.Ft.	$19/Sq.Ft.	$20/Sq.Ft.
Adj. for difference in total sq. ft.	$15–$20/Sq.Ft.	$20–$25/Sq.Ft.	$30–$40/Sq.Ft.
Adj. for age difference; use ½% per year—all home price categories			

Note: The amount of adjustment will vary according to the value of the home. A larger adjustment is appropriate for a more expensive home, less for a less expensive home.

The amount of adjustment in the chart above represents the approximate value that the amenities add to the value of the home, not the amount spent on an improvement. So, if you added a bathroom that cost $7,000, the value added to your home may be much lower.

Always adjust the value of the comparables (downward or upward) relative to your property.

FIGURE 5.5 Guide to Entering Data on the Residential Market Data
Analysis Form

Property Address
Found on the property record card or in your field research.

Distance to Subject
Approximate distance from your property (e.g., two blocks).

Sales Price
Obtained from REALTOR®, records in tax office, or valuation company.

Price/Living Area S/F
The sale price divided by the total square footage as shown under "Living Area/SF."

Source of Data
MLS (Multiple Listing Service); see your REALTOR®.

Date of Sale
If the market has been level during the period, no adjustment is needed.

Living Area S/F
Found on the property record card, by measurement, or through the construction office.

Location
The quality of the location; that is, good, average, fair, or poor.

Site/View
Land size or dimensions found on the property record card.

Design and Appeal
Type of design.

Type of Construction
Frame, brick, stone, etc.

Age
Age of improvements found on the property record card.

FIGURE 5.5 Guide to Entering Data on the Residential Market Data
Analysis Form (Continued)

Condition
Subjective opinion; that is, good, average, fair, or poor.

Room Count
Found on the property record card.

Basement
Found on the property record card.

Garage/Carport
Found on the property record card or through inspection.

Porch/Patio
Found on the property record card or through inspection.

Other
Make adjustments for major amenities.

Net Adj.—Total
Add the figures under the column labeled "Adj. +/-."

Indicated Value
Add the "Net adj.—total" figure to the "Sale Price."

Comments
Comment on the significant differences between the three comparables
and the subject property.

Indicated Value by Market Data Analysis
Select a figure using the three indicated values. If one comparable is
very close to your property in most respects, choose a value slightly
above it. Never choose a value below the lowest value or above the
highest value.

Value per S/F
Divide the "Indicated Value by Market Data Analysis" by the "Living Area
S/F" of your home. Again, the figure used should be slightly above the
lowest figure shown for "Price/Liv. Area S/F."

FIGURE 5.6   Example—Residential Market Data Analysis

	Subject	Comp. #1		Comp. #2		Comp. #3	
Property Address	1313 Reed	1223 Reed		317 Manor		1306 Mason	
Distance to Subject		w/in 1 block		w/in 4 blocks		w/in 5 blocks	
Sales Price	$185,425*	$170,500		$174,500		$169,500	
Price/Liv. Area S/F	$77.26	$71.04		$69.80		$72.12	
Source of Data	Assessor	MLS		MLS		MLS	
	Description	Descrip.	Adj.±	Descrip.	Adj.±	Descrip.	Adj.±
Date of Sale and							
Adjustment/Time	1-1-98	4-12-98		12-20-97		10-13-97	
Living Area S/F	2,400	2,400		2,500	-1000	2,350	+500
Location	Good	Good		Good		Good	
Site/View	1 acre	1 acre		1 acre		1 acre	
Design and Appeal	2 story	2 story		2 story		2 story	
Quality/Construction	Brick	Brick		Brick		Brick	
Age	25	24		23		26	
Condition	Average	Average		Average		Average	
Room Count							
Total	8	9		7		8	
Bedrooms	4	4		4		4	
Baths	2 1/2	2 1/2		2	+1000	1 1/2	+1500
Basement							
Finished						Yes	
Unfinished	Yes	Yes		Yes		No	-3500
Garage/Carport	2 car att.	2 car att.		3 car att.	-2000	1 car att.	+2000
Porch/Patio	Deck	Patio		Deck		Porch	+500
Other							
Swimming Pool							
Fireplace	Yes	None	+1200	Yes		Yes	
Kitchen Equip.							
Remodeling							
Air-Conditioning							
			±		±		±
Net Adj. – Total			+1200		-2000		+1000
Indicated Value		$171,700		$172,500		$170,500	

Comments: All sales are similar in location and style and indicate a narrow adjusted-value range. Sale #1 is nearest the subject in location and size. Sale #2 is slightly larger, indicating a lower s/f value. Sale #3 is slightly smaller, indicating a higher s/f value. All sales were given equal consideration to arrive at a final value estimate.

Indicated Value by Market Data Analysis   **$172,000**

or **$71.66 per S/F**

*The Sales Price and Price/Living Area for the subject are values set by the assessor, not by the actual sale of the subject. In this column, Sales Price is really the market value set by the assessor.

FIGURE 5.7   Example—Residential Market Data Analysis—Subject Property

RESIDENTIAL MARKET DATA ANALYSIS

Subject Property

Legal Description:

_____
_____
_____
_____
_____
_____
_____

PASTE UP PHOTO OF YOUR HOME

Assessor's Property
Identification #:

_____
_____
_____

	Subject	Comp. #1	Comp. #2	Comp. #3
Property Address				
Distance to Subj.				
Sales Price	$_____	$_____	$_____	$_____
Price/Liv. Area S/F	$_____	$_____	$_____	$_____
Source of Data				

	Description	Description	Adj. ±	Description	Adj. ±	Description	Adj. ±
Date of Sale and Adjustment/Time							
Living Area S/F							
Location							
Site/View							
Design and Appeal							
Quality/Constr.							
Age							
Condition							
Room Count							
Total							
Bedrooms							
Baths							
Basement							
Finished							
Unfinished							
Garage/Carport							
Porch/Patio							
Other							
Swimming Pool							
Fireplace							
Kitchen Equip.							
Remodeling							
Air-conditioning							
			±		±		±
Net Adj.—Total							
Indicated Value	$	$		$		$	

Comments: _____

Indicated Value by Market Data Analysis _____ $_____

or $ _____ per S/F

FIGURE 5.8   Example—Residential Market Data Analysis—Comparable Property #1

RESIDENTIAL MARKET DATA ANALYSIS

Comparable Property #1

Legal Description:

PASTE UP PHOTO OF HOME COMP. #1

Assessor's Property
Identification #:

		Comp. #1	
Property Address			
Distance to Subj.			
Sales Price		$	
Price/Liv. Area S/F		$	
Source of Data			
		Description	Adj. ±
Date of Sale and Adjustment/Time			
Living Area S/F			
Location			
Site/View			
Design and Appeal			
Quality/Constr.			
Age			
Condition			
Room Count			
Total			
Bedrooms			
Baths			
Basement			
Finished			
Unfinished			
Garage/Carport			
Porch/Patio			
Other			
Swimming Pool			
Fireplace			
Kitchen Equip.			
Remodeling			
Air-conditioning			
			±
Net Adj.—Total			
Indicated Value		$	

FIGURE 5.9   Example—Residential Market Data Analysis—Comparable Property #2

RESIDENTIAL MARKET DATA ANALYSIS
Comparable Property #2

Legal Description:

PASTE UP PHOTO OF HOME COMP. #2

Assessor's Property
Identification #:

		Comp. #2	
Property Address			
Distance to Subj.			
Sales Price		$	
Price/Liv. Area S/F		$	
Source of Data			
		Description	Adj. ±
Date of Sale and Adjustment/Time			
Living Area S/F			
Location			
Site/View			
Design and Appeal			
Quality/Constr.			
Age			
Condition			
Room Count			
Total			
Bedrooms			
Baths			
Basement			
Finished			
Unfinished			
Garage/Carport			
Porch/Patio			
Other			
Swimming Pool			
Fireplace			
Kitchen Equip.			
Remodeling			
Air-conditioning			
			±
Net Adj.—Total			
Indicated Value		$	

FIGURE 5.10   Example—Residential Market Data Analysis—Comparable Property #3

RESIDENTIAL MARKET DATA ANALYSIS
Comparable Property #3

Legal Description:

_____

_____

_____

_____

_____

_____

_____

PASTE UP PHOTO OF HOME COMP. #3

Assessor's Property
Identification #:

_____

_____

_____

		Comp. #3	
Property Address			
Distance to Subj.			
Sales Price		$	
Price/Liv. Area S/F		$	
Source of Data			
		Description	Adj. ±
Date of Sale and Adjustment/Time			
Living Area S/F			
Location			
Site/View			
Design and Appeal			
Quality/Constr.			
Age			
Condition			
Room Count			
Total			
Bedrooms			
Baths			
Basement			
Finished			
Unfinished			
Garage/Carport			
Porch/Patio			
Other			
Swimming Pool			
Fireplace			
Kitchen Equip.			
Remodeling			
Air-conditioning			
			±
Net Adj.—Total			
Indicated Value		$	

Residential Equity Analysis Approach

This approach entails obtaining comparables for three homes that are located near your property. If you are only using the equity analysis method in your challenge, these homes do not have to have been sold recently. If you are also using the market analysis method, obtain sales and assessment data for each comparable. Assessment information and property record cards are needed for all comparables and the subject. Try to obtain them from the tax assessor's office. If you are unable to do so, you may have to measure the properties yourself or talk to the owners to gather the needed data. You can also visit the local construction/engineer's or planning office to obtain square-footage figures and information about improvements or amenities.

Adjust the values of the three comparables relative to the subject property to arrive at an equitable assessment for your property. Make adjustments for the same items shown on the market analysis approach (e.g., size, bathrooms, fireplaces, garages, air conditioning, etc.) Also obtain current adjustment figures from a local REALTOR® or appraiser.

Record all the information on the blank residential equity analysis record forms found in Figures 5.14 through 5.17 (see also forms in Appendix C). Use the examples in Figures 5.12 and 5.13 as guides for completing the forms. Remember that the adjustments shown are only examples and may not be representative of your area. You must research the appropriate dollar adjustments to use in your area.

CHECK FOR IMPROPER ASSESSMENTS AND RECORD ERRORS

Now that you've examined the possibility of an overassessment on your property, you should look at whether there are any problems with an illegal assessment, an unequal assessment, or record errors.

Let's look first at illegal assessments. Review the list in Chapter 1 of areas that you may challenge. For example, check to see if your assessment is higher than the legal percentage, or higher than the sales assessment ratio. Maybe your property is classified as something other than a residential property.

FIGURE 5.14   Residential Equity Analysis—Subject Property

RESIDENTIAL EQUITY ANALYSIS

Subject Property

Legal Description:

PASTE UP PHOTO OF YOUR HOME

Assessor's Property
Identification #:

Property Address	Subject	Comp. #1	Comp. #2	Comp. #3
Distance to Subj.				
Sales Price	$	$	$	$
Price/Liv. Area S/F	$	$	$	$
Source of Data				
	Description	Description Adj. ±	Description Adj. ±	Description Adj. ±
Date of Sale and Adjustment/Time				
Living Area S/F				
Location				
Site/View				
Design and Appeal				
Quality/Constr.				
Age				
Condition				
Room Count				
Total				
Bedrooms				
Baths				
Basement				
Finished				
Unfinished				
Garage/Carport				
Porch/Patio				
Other				
Swimming Pool				
Fireplace				
Kitchen Equip.				
Remodeling				
Air-conditioning				
Net Adj.—Total		±	±	±
Indicated Value	$	$	$	$

Comments: _____

Indicated Value by Equity Analysis $ _____

or $ _____ per S/F

FIGURE 5.15   Residential Equity Analysis—Comparable Property #1

RESIDENTIAL EQUITY ANALYSIS

Comparable Property #1

Legal Description:

PASTE UP PHOTO OF HOME COMP. #1

Assessor's Property
Identification #:

		Comp. #1	
Property Address			
Distance to Subj.			
Sales Price		$	
Price/Liv. Area S/F		$	
Source of Data			
		Description	Adj. ±
Date of Sale and			
Adjustment/Time			
Living Area S/F			
Location			
Site/View			
Design and Appeal			
Quality/Constr.			
Age			
Condition			
Room Count			
Total			
Bedrooms			
Baths			
Basement			
Finished			
Unfinished			
Garage/Carport			
Porch/Patio			
Other			
Swimming Pool			
Fireplace			
Kitchen Equip.			
Remodeling			
Air-conditioning			±
Net Adj.—Total			
Indicated Value		$	

FIGURE 5.16   Residential Equity Analysis—Comparable Property #2

RESIDENTIAL EQUITY ANALYSIS
Comparable Property #2

PASTE UP PHOTO OF HOME COMP. #2

Legal Description:

Assessor's Property
Identification #:

		Comp. #2
Property Address		
Distance to Subj.		
Sales Price		
Price/Liv. Area S/F		$
Source of Data		$
		Description **Adj. ±**
Date of Sale and		
Adjustment/Time		
Living Area S/F		
Location		
Site/View		
Design and Appeal		
Quality/Constr.		
Age		
Condition		
Room Count		
Total		
Bedrooms		
Baths		
Basement		
Finished		
Unfinished		
Garage/Carport		
Porch/Patio		
Other		
Swimming Pool		
Fireplace		
Kitchen Equip.		
Remodeling		
Air-conditioning		
Net Adj.—Total		±
Indicated Value		$

FIGURE 5.17 Residential Equity Analysis—Comparable Property #3

RESIDENTIAL EQUITY ANALYSIS
Comparable Property #3

Legal Description:

_____

_____

_____

_____

_____

_____

PASTE UP PHOTO OF HOME COMP. #3

Assessor's Property
Identification #:

_____

_____

_____

_____

		Comp. #3	
Property Address			
Distance to Subj.			
Sales Price		$	
Price/Liv. Area S/F		$	
Source of Data			
		Description	**Adj. ±**
Date of Sale and			
Adjustment/Time			
Living Area S/F			
Location			
Site/View			
Design and Appeal			
Quality/Constr.			
Age			
Condition			
Room Count			
Total			
Bedrooms			
Baths			
Basement			
Finished			
Unfinished			
Garage/Carport			
Porch/Patio			
Other			
Swimming Pool			
Fireplace			
Kitchen Equip.			
Remodeling			
Air-conditioning			±
Net Adj.—Total			
Indicated Value		$	

Next, look for an unequal assessment, an assessment higher than market value. You may have even recently purchased your property for less than the assessed value. Look for these situations and write them down.

Also, search for errors on your property record card. Check the assessor's manual to verify that the correct factors were used. Check every calculation shown on your record card, and look for other errors, such as those shown in Figures 5.18 and 5.19.

CONDOMINIUM OR TOWN HOUSE

If your residence is a condominium or town house and you want to attempt to reduce your property taxes, your approach will be similar to what we have already discussed. The difference will be in the analysis of comparable properties. You may want to use a sales ratio approach where you'll compare the assessed value of each property to the sales price for condominiums or town houses, similar to yours, that have been sold within the last year or during the assessment period. For example, suppose you own Model A in a condominium development. First you will need to identify other Model A units in that development that have sold within the assessment period. Then you calculate the ratio of the assessed value for each one to its sales price. Next, you compute an average for all of the comparables. You can also effectively use the standard market approach to prove your case by selecting three comparable sales in your development, making adjustments, and determining what the assessed value of your property should be. You may want to examine both approaches and decide which one presents your case in a more favorable light.

The sales ratio study in Figure 5.20 illustrates the ratio method.

FIGURE 5.18   Sample Property Record Card

PROPERTY RECORD CARD

Township _FAIRFAX_   Taxing District _UP_   Section or Plat _____ Block _M_ Lot _4_

Property Address _16 W. MAIN ST._   Property Class _R_

Owner Name _JOHN & MARY JONES_

Owner Address _SAME_

Property Description:

      ENGLEWOOD SUBDIVISION

      CORNER LOT

Assessment Record

Yr	Land	23420
	Bldgs	69 073
	Total	92493

Yr	Land	
	Bldgs	
	Total	

Property Factors

Topography	Improvements	Streets	District
Level ____	City Wtr. _X_	Pvd. _X_	Impr. _X_
High ____	Sewer _X_	Unimp. ____	Stat. ____
Low ____	Gas ____	Sidwlk. _X_	Decl. ____
Rolling _x_	Elect. _X_		Blight ____
Swampy ____	All util. ____		

Yr	Land	
	Bldgs	
	Total	

Yr	Land	
	Bldgs	
	Total	

Building Permits

Date	Number	Amount	Purpose
8/97	1234	$3500	DECK

Yr	Land	
	Bldgs	
	Total	

Land Value Computations

Frontage	Depth	Unit Value	Depth Factor	Act. Value	True Value	Assessed Value
120	75	50	1-14	57	46840	

Yr	Land	
	Bldgs	
	Total	

Total Land Value 46840 23420
Total Bldg Value 138146 69073
Total Value—Bldgs and Land 184986 92493

Yr	Land	
	Bldgs	
	Total	

FIGURE 5.19   Sample Building Record

BUILDING RECORD		

Occupancy
Vacant Lot _____
Building ___Ẍ___   Qty. _1_

Plumbing
Standard ___Ẍ___   Nonstand. __
Baths   1 __ 2 Ẍ 3 __ 4 __
Kitchen __MODERN__
Laundry ___Ẍ___
Water Heater ___Ẍ___

Basement
Finished _____ Unfinished _FULL_

Heating & Air-conditioning
Central Air ___Ẍ___
Hot Water/Steam _____
Electric _____
Unit heaters _____
Oil Forced Air ___Ẍ___
Gas _____

Exterior Walls
Brick ____ Stone ____ Block __
Frame _Ẍ_ Other _____

Floors   B   1   2   3
Concrete   Ẍ
Wood   __   X   Ẍ   __
Tile   __   __ __ __

Interior finish
Dry wall ___Ẍ___
Other _____
Unfinished _____

Nbr. of rooms   B   1   2   3
          __   5   3   __

Other features
Fireplaces _Ẍ (1)_
Other _____

Dwelling Computations

	Unit	Amount
	_1520_ S/F	_1,30 400_
A/C		_20 50_
Attic		
Garage		_37 00_
Other		
Other		
Subtotal 1		_1,36150_
Grade factor		_1.24_
Subtotal 2		_168826_
Cty. factor		_1.16_
Repl. value		_195838_
Depreciation		_02_
True Value		_191921_

Age _1997_
Date _8/98_

Dimensions on sketch: 15, 22, 20, 50, 30, 26

FIGURE 5.20   Sales Ratio Study—Valleybrook Condominiums Block 36

| Lot | Year Built | 1999 Assessed Value (Figs. in 1,000s) | | | Sales Price (Figs. in 1,000s) Sales | | Date | Ratio AV/SP |
		Land	Improv	Total	Model A	Model B		
5.05	1997	$71.3	$140.1	$ 211.4	$ 235.0		11/08/98	89.96%
5.08	1996	$75.9	$160.4	$ 236.3		$280.0	12/12/98	84.39%
5.17	1997	$75.0	$140.1	$ 215.1	$ 277.0		12/15/98	77.65%
5.18	1996	$75.0	$140.1	$ 215.1	$ 269.9		3/09/99	79.70%
5.21	1997	$75.9	$162.4	$ 238.3		$290.0	7/15/99	82.17%
5.23	1997	$75.0	$140.1	$ 215.1	$ 254.5		1/10/99	84.52%
5.45	1997	$75.0	$145.3	$ 220.3	$ 252.3		10/27/98	87.32%
5.54	1997	$75.0	$147.8	$ 222.8		$283.0	3/31/99	78.73%
5.56	1997	$75.9	$140.1	$ 216.0	$ 258.5		9/16/99	83.56%
Totals				$1990.4	$1547.2	$853.0		748.00%
No. of Sales				9	6	3		9
Mean Sales Price					$ 257.9	$284.3		
Mean Assessment				$ 221.2	$ 215.5	$232.5		
Mean Sales Ratio (AV/SP)					83.56%	81.78%		83.11%

Notes:

1. All units have a two-car garage, basement, fireplace, two bedrooms, frame construction, and were built in 1996 and 1997.
2. Square footage of Model A is 2161; Model B is 2641.
3. Square footage figures exclude garage and basement.
4. Only sales between 10/15/98 and 10/14/99 were included because those dates coincide with the figures used by the tax assessor for the tax year.

Terms Used in the Sales Ratio Study

- *Block.* The number assigned to the block that represents the area in which the condominiums/town houses are located as shown on the tax map.
- *Lot.* The lot number assigned to each individual condominium/town house property as identified on the tax map.
- *Assessed Value.* Assessed value determined by the tax assessor for tax purposes. Three figures are shown: one for the assessed value of the land, one for the value of the improvements thereon (e.g., the condominium building), and the total of the two figures.
- *AV/SP.* Assessed value (AV) divided by the sales price (SP).
- *No. of Sales.* The number of sales included in the column.
- *Mean Sales Price (average sales price).* Totals of all the sale prices divided by the number of sales shown for that model.
- *Mean Assessment (average assessed value).* Sum of the figure shown under the heading, "Assessed Value–Total" ($1990.4) and "Sales Price-Model A" ($1547.2) and Model B ($853.0) divided by the respective number of sales (9,6, or 3) shown under each. For example, $1990.4 ÷ 9 = $221.2, or $1547.2 ÷ 6 = $257.9, etc.
- *Mean Sales Ratio.* The figures shown in the "Sales Price" columns represent the "Mean Assessment" divided by the "Mean Sales Price." In the "Ratio AV/SP" column, the "Mean Sales Ratio" is derived by dividing the total of all the ratios by the number of sales. Thus, it is the average of both models added together.

Let's assume that the subject property in our example is located on lot 5.10, is a Model A unit, and has an assessed value of $221,000. It is similar in all respects to the units shown in the study. If we had purchased the unit for $258,500, and we applied the mean sales ratio to that figure, the assessed value should be about $216,000 ($258,500 × 83.56% or .8356 = $216,002.60). Thus, we would ask the assessor to lower our assessed value to that figure. If we had been living in the unit for several years, so that there had been no recent sale of the subject property, we could request a reduction to the "mean assessment" amount that we calculated in our study to be $215,500.

In either case, the amount of reduction in actual taxes paid would be small. If the reduction in assessed value was only $5,000, and the tax rate was $1.05 per $100 of assessed value, a savings of only $52.50 per year would result. You will, however, enjoy this saving each year until another valuation is done in your community. The objective is to determine whether you are being taxed fairly and equitably. In this example the taxation was close to an equitable amount, but a small reduction can still be had.

In some states, an appeal may be made by the condominium association on behalf of the individual owners, provided that the condominium declaration allows for the association to appeal taxes as a group when there is a majority vote to do so. If this is the approach used, you should conduct a sales ratio study on another condominium development similar to yours that is located nearby. A comparison of the mean sales ratios for both developments should be done. If the other development has the lowest ratios, your development is paying higher taxes based on a comparison between sales and assessed values. Be certain, however, that the square footages of the developments are similar and that there are no significant differences between the units in both developments.

For a cooperative (co-op) arrangement, where the cooperative association owns the building(s) and leases space to the shareholders of the association (the theoretical owners of each co-op apartment), a sales ratio study should be done to compare the entire building to another similar co-op building in the same geographic area.

FINAL THOUGHTS

Remember that details are important when compiling the data you will use for your tax appeal. Be sure to double-check your figures.

Researching your appeal is the most important part of preparing your tax appeal case. You must proceed carefully and probe all possible areas for tax relief. If you don't find a problem, the assessor will not likely bring any to your attention.

Keep complete lists of everything you find. Compile information on one record so you won't overlook anything at appeal time.

Use the checklist in Step 1 so that you don't overlook any important items to examine. A thorough job of analysis is vital to your appeal.

Look for errors in these areas:

- ☐ *Check the property factors.* Are they accurate?
- ☐ *Check the depth factor used.* The correct factor can be found in the assessor's manual.
- ☐ *Check the unit value.* Is it fair compared to similar sites?
- ☐ *Check the land dimensions.* Are they correct?
- ☐ *Check the computations.* Were the calculations done accurately?
- ☐ *Check the assessed value.* Was it calculated properly according to the assessor's manual? Is the assessed value the correct percentage prescribed by your state?

▼ Remember, checking for mathematical errors is one of the most important things you can do when preparing for a tax appeal. It will benefit you immensely in most cases because the records are full of errors.

Frequently Asked *Q*uestions

Q. What is a comparable?

A. For property tax appeal purposes, it is a house, similar to yours in size, style, location, amenities and year of construction, that sold within the assessment period.

Q. What's the best way to find comparable properties?

A. Contact a local REALTOR® or appraiser, or visit the tax assessor's office. These sources will often have a computer that can access lists of properties sold in your area, or they can find the information in their own records.

Q. Why should I take pictures of my property and the comparables I use?

A. A picture can help you focus in on the characteristics of your house that you want the assessor to see (e.g., a crack in the wall, peeling paint, or damage from a leaking roof). Use photos to your advantage whenever possible. Photos significantly enable you to present your case in a professional manner, and they illustrate the specific points you want to emphasize in your presentation. Photos of comparables accomplish the same task.

Q. Why should I use a Residential Market Data Analysis form to present my findings?

A. A form helps you organize your materials so you can present them in a logical, effective manner. It also appears more professional and lets the tax assessor know you have done your homework and know what you're talking about.

Q. Why are the values used for making adjustments so different from the real values in the marketplace?

A. When a bathroom or kitchen is remodeled, the amount you put into the remodeling may be fully regained when you sell the property. It's not a dollar-for-dollar arrangement. A willing buyer is not going to match every cent you spent for remodeling. So, the adjustment values will vary, sometimes significantly, from what was actually spent. The actual price per square foot paid for a property may be much higher than the value you will use to make an adjustment.

Preparing Your Tax Appeal

KEY POINTS TO REMEMBER WHEN PREPARING YOUR HOMEOWNER'S TAX APPEAL

Your goal is to gather data that will show the lowest valid assessed value for your property. Therefore, always look for comparables with lower assessed values and/or market values than your property.

Market value is normally the best indicator of value for a residence. Therefore, if you use this approach, along with support from any other approaches, such as cost or equity, then more weight will be given to the conclusions you reach.

> The best indicator of value for a residence is generally market value. Be sure to research sold properties in your subdivision similar to yours to find the ones with the lowest assessed value that will best illustrate that your assessed value should be reduced.

Your objective when presenting facts about cost, market, or equity is to use the figures to prove that the value of your property is lower than the value shown on the property record card. Always select the approach, or approaches, that show the value of your property in the most unfavorable light—in other words, the lowest value.

When gathering sales data, make sure that the sale was a "usable" one. Transfers of convenience, sales that convey only part of the property, sales to or from charitable institutions, transactions where the full consideration was minimal, or transfers within a family are example of possible "nonusable" sales. Avoid them.

> ▼ Make sure that the sales you use for your tax appeal are usable sales. Check with the tax assessor's office to be sure the comparables you selected are usable, and find out how a usable property is defined.

When using the equity approach, the comparables must be within the same taxing jurisdiction as your property. With the market data approach, this is not required. However, if you plan to submit data using both approaches, the comparables you use should match. Therefore, use properties within the same taxing jurisdiction.

In some states, the taxing jurisdiction can raise your assessed value as a result of your appeal, so be careful to analyze your data thoroughly before filing an appeal. Be certain that you aren't underassessed.

If the data you gather does not support filing an appeal, examine your situation again the following year. You may find that you have a valid case at that time. Remember, many factors affect your assessed value, so review them frequently to find information that will support an appeal.

> ▼ Even if your first analysis of your assessed value doesn't yield a strong case, do it again the following year and every year in which the assessed values change. It will eventually pay off for you.

If your case goes to tax court, visit the court before you present your case to observe how the proceedings are conducted, and what the members of the tax board talk about during the appeal of a case to get a general feeling for what you can expect when you appear.

When preparing to negotiate with the tax assessor or members of the court, remember the rules of successful negotiating. Let the assessor make the first offer, and never say yes too quickly.

The tax assessor is under a legal obligation to be fair and not litigious when providing you with information. The courts also view the homeowner as competent to testify about the value of his or her residence, so don't lack confidence when presenting your case. You probably know more about your house than the tax assessor or the court.

Before going to the tax court with an appeal, obtain a copy of the rules of the court by calling your local administrative offices. Review them and be sure you understand and follow them when presenting your case.

In a sense, the tax collection system is a political one. You should use this to your advantage. One way to do this is to solicit the help of your neighbors who may also feel unfairly taxed. There is strength in numbers. Consider making an appeal as a unified group. Share information with your neighbors. Read the newspapers and talk with your friends and neighbors about what is going on in the property tax arena.

Also be aware that in some states, it is illegal to raise property taxes for a specified period after an addition or change to the property. In some jurisdictions, this period may last until the next revaluation is completed. If you've made significant changes or improvements, check with your assessor to determine the rules in your area.

Use the following checklist to ensure you've done everything necessary for a successful tax appeal.

Homeowner's Property Tax Appeal Checklist

Check each box when completed. For a market data analysis:

☐ All comparables are located in the same general area as your property and are similar in age and design.

☐ All comparables were sold during the assessment period in your state. Use the comparables sold closest to the cutoff date for the assessment period or those sold within a six-month period prior to that date.

☐ You adjusted the comparables to reflect the amenities of your property.

☐ You used current figures for your area to make adjustments.

☐ All sales shown were "usable."

☐ Your comparables have lower assessed values per square foot than your property.

☐ You concluded your analysis with a suggested value.

☐ Your suggested value is higher than the lowest comparable value.

☐ Your suggested value was closest to the adjusted value of the comparable with the least adjustments.

For a cost analysis:

☐ You used this approach to value because current sales data weren't available.

☐ You used the current cost figures for your area when making cost adjustments.

☐ You sought the assistance of a competent appraiser or REALTOR® to obtain cost values and to help you with your analysis.

For an equity analysis:

☐ You have checked to determine whether an equity analysis is acceptable in your state.

☐ The comparables you used are within the same taxing jurisdiction.

☐ If you also use a market analysis, the comparables used in the equity analysis match those in the market analysis.

When looking for an illegal assessment, was

☐ your property assessed at more than the legal assessment?
☐ your property not inspected by the assessor?
☐ the wrong approach to value your property used by the assessor?
☐ your assessment higher than the state issued sales-assessment ratio?
☐ your property not assessed within the proper class?
☐ a notice of increased assessment not issued or posted?

When looking for an unequal assessment, was

☐ your property assessed at more than market value?
☐ an assessment on a similar property lower than yours?
☐ your property recently purchased for less than the assessed value?

Also:

☐ Have you checked for mathematical and mechanical errors in your tax records?
☐ Have you determined that the depreciation used for your property was correct?
☐ Have you checked the personal exemptions to which you are entitled?
☐ Have you organized your presentation for the discussion with your tax assessor so that it follows a logical sequence and concludes with a suggested value?
☐ To avoid a tax increase, have you checked that your property is not underassessed before filing your appeal?

Frequently Asked Questions

Q. If a brother sold the house to his sister, why can't I use the sale as a comparable?

A. This is an "unusable" sale because the two relatives may have agreed on a sale price that is not representative of the market values. One or both of them may have an underlying, unrevealed reason for the price agreed upon. Thus, it is generally not considered a valid comparable.

Q. When should I hire a property tax attorney or property tax agent to prepare and present my property tax appeal?

A. One of these experts should be used when you appeal to a higher reviewing body after being rejected or partially turned down at a lower level. An expert should only be hired when you have a strong case and when the potential return justifies the cost of paying for his or her services. Of course, you could always use an expert from the beginning, but you will find that you can do an effective job at the lower levels of appeals without help.

Q. Can I start the appeal process at the board of review level and go from there to a higher level if necessary?

A. No. Appeals are always presented first at the lowest level and then progress through a set sequence of appeal levels. You must always begin at the tax assessor level, and if denied, continue appealing at each successive, prescribed level in the appeal process.

Q. Why should I use the Property Tax Appeal Checklist provided in this chapter?

A. A checklist is a very effective tool to help you avoid overlooking a significant element when preparing and presenting an appeal. I would suggest you always use a checklist to ensure you haven't missed something.

Q. *Why can't I suggest an assessed value for my property that is lower than the range I calculate after applying my adjustment values for differences between the my property and the comparables?*

A. The purpose of applying adjustments to your comparables is to determine a reasonable range of values into which your assessed value should fall. If you get outside of this range, the assessor will likely deny your appeal. Always choose a value within the range. After all, the purpose of making the adjustments is to find a reasonable assessed value for your property. Appraisers adhere to this rule, so you should also.

Presenting Your Tax Appeal

PRESENTING YOUR CASE TO THE ASSESSOR

When you are ready to present your appeal, contact your local assessor and arrange a meeting to discuss your case. When you meet, present your case in a conversational, relaxed manner. Assessors are not to be feared. They are hard working, busy people with strengths and weaknesses just like you.

Your meeting with the assessor should have an informal tone. Be relaxed, but direct and organized in your approach. You are there, in effect, to say: "I've been looking at my property tax situation. After gathering a substantial amount of information, doing a lot of checking, and organizing the facts I've discovered, I feel my assessed value should be lowered. Here's why." There should be no confrontation, merely a presentation of information that justifies your position.

It is important to your success that you be friendly, businesslike, and confident. Keep in mind that you know more about your property and your comparables than the assessor. Be especially careful not to criticize the assessor for any errors you've found. Let the facts speak for themselves.

How you present your data is a matter of personal style and preference. Many experts find that an informal but organized approach is best. This will enable you to control the tone and direction of the discussion and avoid missing any important points that you want to cover. Have a general sequence in mind of what you intend to discuss. Begin with an overview statement, such as, "I have a market analysis, some questions I'd like to ask, and some facts to review that will illustrate why I believe that my taxes are too high. Shall we begin with the set of questions?" This approach gives the assessor a feel for the direction you wish to take, yet it allows you to control the sequence of your presentation. Beginning with a series of questions is nonthreatening and lets you both relax and break the ice.

Next, discuss any discrepancies or errors that you found. For example, if the depreciation factor assigned to your home is less than that of your comparables, you could bring this to the assessor's attention and inquire about the reasons for the difference. To illustrate, let's say that on the property record card a depreciation factor of 5 percent is shown, while 15 percent was used for your comparables. If all properties are the same age, construction, and condition, your neighbors are getting better tax treatment than you. If the cost of your house on the property record card was $125,000 with a 5 percent depreciation factor, the value used to figure your taxes would be 95 percent of $125,000, or $118,750. If one of your comparables has the same cost of $125,000, but a depreciation factor of 15 percent, the assessed value would be $125,000 multiplied by 85 percent, or $106,250. Thus, you are paying taxes on the difference ($118,750 minus $106,250, or $12,500) when you shouldn't be. Here is where you might want to produce good photographs of the comparable homes to convince the assessor that they are in the same condition, and that you are being overtaxed.

> The best way to prove a reduction in your assessed value is needed is through market data. The next best method is to prove mathematical errors or incorrect measurements. Check carefully in these areas.

If you have found other factors that have an impact on the assessed value, such as math errors or differences in depreciation that will lower your assessed value, you should review them with the assessor. Your purpose is to demonstrate how the cost valuation used on the property record card is incorrect. A reduction in this value will lower your tax obligation.

Finally, you should present your market data analysis and/or equity analysis data. You could briefly highlight how you arrived at the final values and conclude your presentation with the value you believe your property should be assessed. Suggesting—and supporting—the value you want is very important. Your analysis will support your conclusion of value and you need to point this out to your assessor. Not suggesting a value allows the assessor to form his or her own conclusion which might not be satisfactory to you.

> Always conclude your discussion with the tax assessor—and any higher reviewing body to which you present your appeal—with a suggested value for your property.

Whenever you make an appeal, keep in mind that the value of a property is partly subjective. It is an opinion that is supported by facts, but there can still be differences of opinion regarding those facts. You may not be in total agreement with the assessor as to the value you have established.

Usually the assessor will tell you that he or she will look at your records and the data you presented and call you in a few days with an opinion. Rarely will a decision be given on the spot, even if one could be given. Don't let that bother you. It's routine.

When you and the assessor meet again, the assessor may offer to settle on a value that is higher than your facts indicate. You can try to negotiate further, but if you are unable to convince the assessor to accept your figure, you must decide if you will settle for the higher valuation. Your alternative is to proceed to the local review board. It might be better to accept a slightly higher valuation than to risk a worse settlement later.

The assessor will usually prefer to make a settlement on his or her level than have to justify the assessment in the presence of superiors in a courtroom atmosphere at the review board hearing. Remember, you can always make another appeal the following year and perhaps achieve a more satisfactory valuation.

If you accept the decision, you will receive a notice of a reduction in assessed value within a week or two.

If the assessor's offer is unfavorable and you choose not to accept it, plan to file a formal appeal. The procedure for a formal appeal is described later in this chapter.

If you win a new assessed value, your mortgage company will be notified that your tax bill has been reduced. They then will send you a statement that may give you the option of a reduced monthly payment or to have the excess dollars collected placed in an escrow account to be applied toward later tax increases.

HOW TO PRESENT YOUR APPEAL TO THE REVIEW BOARD

The review board usually consists of three to five people who, depending on your state, are either appointed or elected to the board. Often they are people with varied backgrounds, but many have been or are involved in the real estate field, or serve in some other government capacity.

There may be two ways in which to present your case to the assessment review board:

1. You may be allowed to submit a grievance statement along with supporting documents without having to appear before the board.
2. The property owner and/or a designated person may be permitted to support the written statement before the board. The support person may be a property tax attorney or a property tax consultant. A consultant may act as an expert witness, but may not always be allowed to represent the client in a legal capacity. A lawyer may represent the client and act as an expert witness. Check your local laws by calling the tax administration office.

If you represent yourself at the review board hearing, you may want to prepare presentation displays to illustrate your case to the review board. This is a matter of personal style and choice. You may, of course, feel more comfortable just letting your documentation speak for itself. If so, be sure you furnish the board with a copy of all documents to refer to while you present your facts. The board, in most instances, will not make its decision immediately in your presence. Having heard the evidence and read the documents submitted, the board may proceed immediately to the next case and meet privately afterward to resolve all cases. Once a decision is reached, the board will direct the assessor to make whatever changes are determined. Most likely the grievant (you) will not be notified directly of the board's action. The results, however, can be found through the assessor's office.

You have an opportunity once each year to file your appeal. If you miss that chance, you must wait until the following year to make a challenge for tax relief. Therefore, you should check with the tax assessor's office to determine the exact date of the filing period. After all complaints are heard, the final assessment roll must be completed. Once completed, it may be open for public inspection, but taxpayers can no longer file grievances. This public inspection has no particular significance other than to make the public aware of the final assessed values.

JUDICIAL REVIEW

Once you learn the results of the grievance at the local level, you must decide if you are satisfied with the board's decision. If you are not, you may carry the case to a higher court. This may be a special agency, a tax court, or an appeals court. In any case, this higher group has the power to sustain or overturn an assessment made locally.

As with the original grievance procedure, there is a limited time for filing an appeal. This appeal information is accessible through your state's real property tax laws or the Commerce Clearing House Tax Guide.

Whenever you are considering an appeal to a higher court, you might want to consult a qualified property tax attorney to review your case and advise you whether a further appeal is worthwhile. At this level, due to the expense of legal counsel, you should be sure that you have a strong case. Attorneys, however, will work on a contingency basis, charging a fee only if they win your case.

See Figures 7.1 and 7.2 for real property protest procedures.

FIGURE 7.1 Real Property Protest Procedures

REAL PROPERTY PROTEST PROCEDURES
(Land and Buildings or other Improvements to the Land)

(This State's statutes define "improvements" as all structures, buildings, fixtures, fences and water rights erected on or affixed to land, whether or not title to such land has been acquired.)

Protests by Mail: If you choose to mail a written protest, you may elect to complete the attached protest form and mail or FAX it to the Assessor at the address listed on the front of the Notice of Valuation. To preserve your right to protest it <u>must</u> be postmarked no later than _____.

Protests in Person: If you choose to present oral or written objections to the Assessor in person, you may elect to complete the protest form and deliver it to the Assessor at the address listed on the front of the Notice of Valuation. To preserve your right to protest, you <u>must</u> appear in the county Assessor's office on or before _____.

AFTER THESE DATES, YOUR RIGHT TO PROTEST IS LOST

<u>Assessor's Determination:</u> The Assessor must make a decision on your protest and mail a Notice of Determination to you by the **last regular working day in** _____. <u>Appealing the Assessor's Decision:</u> If you are not satisfied with the Assessor's determination regarding your value, or if you do not receive a Notice of Determination from the Assessor, you <u>must file</u> a written appeal with the County Board of Equalization **on or before** _____.

TO PRESERVE YOUR APPEAL RIGHTS, YOU MUST PROVE YOU HAVE FILED A TIMELY APPEAL; THEREFORE, WE RECOMMEND <u>ALL</u> CORRESPONDENCE BE <u>MAILED WITH PROOF OF MAILING.</u>

FOR MORE INFORMATION, CONTACT THE ASSESSOR'S OFFICE AT THE TELEPHONE NUMBER LISTED ON THE NOTICE OF VALUATION.

FIGURE 7.2   Sample Homeowner's Property Tax Appeal Form

REAL PROPERTY PROTEST FORM
YOU MAY ELECT TO COMPLETE THIS FORM
TO PROTEST YOUR PROPERTY VALUATION OR CLASSIFICATION.

REAL PROPERTY VALUATION PROTESTS: If you disagree with the "current year actual value" or the classification determined for your property, you may file a protest by mail or in person with the County Assessor. Please refer to the Protest Procedures located on the reverse side of this form for the deadline dates for filing protests. Completing the Real Property Questionnaire will help you determine an estimate of value for your property, which can be compared to the value determined by the Assessor. This State's law requires consideration of the market approaches to value for residential properties (including apartments) and the cost, market, and income approaches to value for vacant land, commercial, and industrial properties.

DOCUMENTATION - REASON FOR REQUESTING A REVIEW: _____

_____

_____

IF MAILING THIS PROTEST FORM,
PLEASE MAKE A COPY OF THIS FORM FOR YOUR RECORDS

REAL PROPERTY QUESTIONNAIRE
ATTACH ADDITIONAL DOCUMENTS AS NECESSARY

Parcel I.D. Number _____   **Owner Name** _____

MARKET APPROACH: This approach to value uses sales from the appropriate time period to determine the actual value of your property. The following items, if known, will help you estimate the market value of your property. If available, attach a copy of any appraisal or written estimate of value. Have similar properties in your immediate neighborhood sold?

DATE SOLD	PROPERTY ADDRESS	SELLING PRICE

Based on these sales and accounting for differences between sold properties and your property, state the value of your property: $ _____

AGENT ASSIGNMENT: I authorize the below named agent to act on my behalf regarding the property tax valuation of the property described herein for the year _____.

Agent's Name (Please Print): _____   Telephone Number: _____

Owner's Signature: _____   Date: _____

Please mail all correspondence regarding this protest to the above named agent at the following address:

_____

Indicate name and telephone number for a person the Assessor may contact if an on-site inspection is necessary:

Name: _____   Telephone Number: _____

VERIFICATION: I, the undersigned owner or agent of this property, state that the information and facts contained herein and on any attachment constitute true and complete statements concerning the described property.

Signature: _____   Date: _____

Frequently Asked *Q*uestions

Q. What is the most effective way to present my property tax appeal?

A. Prepare a list of the errors you have found, use an analysis form to record your comparables information and adjustments, use photographs of each comparable and your property, and present all your information in a logical, straightforward manner. Avoid criticizing the tax assessor, be polite and nonconfrontational, and smile whenever possible. You're talking to a live person, one who may not have had anything to do with calculating your assessed value, but has *everything* to do with the success of your appeal. So do it right!

Q. When I'm selecting comparables, what size house can I use?

Whenever possible, stick with comparable homes that are no more than 20 percent smaller or larger in square footage than your own home. In fact, 10 percent would be a better standard to use, with 20 percent as the limit. The reason is that a home 20 percent larger than yours appeals to a completely different buyer. That buyer may be willing to pay more per square foot for the right home, or factors in his or her selection may be totally different from those involving your property.

Q. Why should I use an equity analysis form in addition to my market data analysis form?

A. The best indicator of value for residential, owner-occupied properties is market data. However, a summary of the differences in assessed values and the resulting property taxes for your comparables helps to support the market data. It also helps you spot significant problem areas on the property record cards.

Q. *What should I do if the tax assessor offers a partial reduction in my assessed value?*

A. That depends on your situation and the answer is different in every case. Let's say, for example, that you think the assessed value should be $150,000 on a house with an assessed value of $225,000. But the assessor offers you a reduction in assessed value to $175,000. You can take the money and run or appeal to a higher court. But is it worth it? What are your chances of getting a greater reduction at a higher level? What would happen if the board of review decided that the value should be $185,000—$10,000 higher than the assessor thought it should be? The factors you need to consider are the risk, the chances of winning, and additional costs you might incur if you appeal higher.

Q. *Why can't I mail in my appeal and be done with it?*

A. You can. However, if your appeal gets delayed in the mail system and you miss the deadline for filing, you may have to wait a considerable amount of time before you can appeal again. Your appeal might even get lost in the mail. More importantly, when you present your appeal in person, you have a better chance of winning your case. You are face to face with the staff member in the tax assessor's office and you can establish a rapport with that person. That can help you win your case. Also, by presenting your appeal in person, your effort and professionalism will come across more clearly. That can also impact how the staff member views your appeal and could be enough to sway him or her to rule in your favor.

Enjoying Your Win!

If you have put forth the effort to properly analyze your property tax situation and decided to appeal your taxes for valid reasons, congratulations are in order. You have probably won your appeal—an accomplishment you may never have thought possible.

Although you may have spent several hours looking for comparables, gathering data, and preparing and presenting your case, you should feel satisfaction in what you have achieved. And should you acquire another residence in the future, you now know enough about the property tax system to do it again.

> Would you ignore balancing your checkbook? Probably not—at least not every month! Entry clerks occasionally make errors. The same can happen with your property record card. So check it carefully on an annual basis.

In addition to feeling satisfied, your work will pay off for years to come in the tax reduction that you've won. It could save you hundreds, perhaps thousands of dollars!

YOUR HOMEOWNER'S LIFETIME PROPERTY TAX SAVINGS CALCULATOR

Your Homeowner's Lifetime Property Tax Savings Calculator (shown in Figure 8.1) offers visual insight into the realm of winning a property tax appeal. A win of any size is cumulative, building on itself each year. The money saved will compound as you allocate the sum to investments which accrue to your interest—not the tax collector's. There are few exercises in the management of our personal lives which contain more opportunity for financial gain.

The longer you own your home, the greater your return will be. In the example in Figure 8.1, a 10 percent downward adjustment, due to challenged assessments on a modest $3,000 tax bill, creates an annual tax savings of $300. The projection for continued ownership of 10 years results in a $3,000 tax savings—an enormous reward for this homeowner.

You can clip and reproduce blank copies of this calculator form for your own projections and lifetime records. A master copy appears in Figure 8.2, and in Appendix C.

YOUR HOMEOWNER'S LIFETIME PROPERTY ASSESSMENT TAX RECORD

Annual posting of your homeowner's lifetime property assessment tax record makes possible an instant visual comparison of the assessed valuations plus the actual real property taxes paid for the current year and the previous year. Answers to high priority questions are highlighted. Have real property taxes been increased this year, because of

- increased levels of government service?
- increased cost of government service?
- increased assessed valuation?

FIGURE 8.1 Your Homeowner's Lifetime Property Tax Savings Calculator

How Much Will You Save?

This Year's Tax Assessment	Select One	Projected % Cut	=	Projected $ Cut	Select One	# of Years	=	Projected Tax Savings
	X	1	=	30.00	X	1	=	
	X	2	=	60.00	X	2	=	
	X	3	=	90.00	X	3	=	
	X	4	=	120.00	X	4	=	
	X	5	=	150.00	X	5	=	
	X	6	=	180.00	X	6	=	
	X	7	=	210.00	X	7	=	
	X	8	=	240.00	X	8	=	
	X	9	=	270.00	X	9	=	
3,000.00	X	10	=	300.00	X	10	=	3,000.00
	X	11	=	330.00	X	11	=	
	X	12	=	360.00	X	12	=	
	X	13	=	390.00	X	13	=	
	X	14	=	420.00	X	14	=	
	X	15	=	450.00	X	15	=	
	X	16	=	480.00	X	16	=	
	X	17	=	510.00	X	17	=	
	X	18	=	540.00	X	18	=	
	X	19	=	570.00	X	19	=	
	X	20	=	600.00	X	20	=	
	X	21	=	630.00	X	21	=	
	X	22	=	660.00	X	22	=	
	X	23	=	690.00	X	23	=	
	X	24	=	720.00	X	24	=	
	X	25	=	750.00	X	25	=	
						30	=	

Example: To get familiar with these easy-to-use calculations, look at the projection we selected above:

	$3,000.00	This year's tax assessment
X	10	Projected % cut in tax assessment
=	$300.00	Projected $ cut in tax assessment
x	10	Projected years of ownership
=	$3,000.00	Projected tax savings due to challenged assessment

FIGURE 8.2   Your Homeowner's Lifetime Property Tax Savings Calculator

How Much Will You Save?

This Year's Tax Assessment	Select One	Projected % Cut	=	Projected $ Cut	Select One	# of Years	=	Projected Tax Savings
	X	1	=		X	1	=	
	X	2	=		X	2	=	
	X	3	=		X	3	=	
	X	4	=		X	4	=	
	X	5	=		X	5	=	
	X	6	=		X	6	=	
	X	7	=		X	7	=	
	X	8	=		X	8	=	
	X	9	=		X	9	=	
	X	10	=		X	10	=	
	X	11	=		X	11	=	
	X	12	=		X	12	=	
	X	13	=		X	13	=	
	X	14	=		X	14	=	
	X	15	=		X	15	=	
	X	16	=		X	16	=	
	X	17	=		X	17	=	
	X	18	=		X	18	=	
	X	19	=		X	19	=	
	X	20	=		X	20	=	
	X	21	=		X	21	=	
	X	22	=		X	22	=	
	X	23	=		X	23	=	
	X	24	=		X	24	=	
	X	25	=		X	25	=	
						30	=	

The example in Figure 8.3 provides an instant answer: The tax rate is equal for the comparison years; therefore, the extra $168 in taxes paid is caused by the total assessed valuation being increased by 14 percent for the year.

You are in a better position to determine the fairness of your assessment by posting this record each year. If it appears equitable, fine. If not, perhaps an assessment appeal is in order.

> One of the most important reasons to keep a continuing record of your tax appeal accomplishments is that the record reveals changes, such as a new market or assessed value, that can trigger you to re-examine your individual situation and get another reduction.

You can clip and reproduce blank copies of this form for your own lifetime records. A master copy appears in Figure 8.4, and in Appendix C.

Frequently Asked *Q*uestions

Q. Why should I keep a record of what I did on each appeal?

A. Keeping a record helps you to see changes in assessed values. Also, it gives you a sense of accomplishment, even if you don't have a case. And when you win a case, it makes you feel great to review what you did. It also has value by allowing you to see how much money you are saving over the years you remain in your home.

FIGURE 8.3 Your Homeowner's Lifetime Property Assessment Tax Record

Example: **1998 Homestead View**

Last Year: **This Year:**

Description	Last Year's Assessed Valuation	Last Year's %	This Year's Assessed Valuation	This Year's %	$ Valuation (+) Change <->	% Valuation (+) Change <->	Last Year's Tax Rate	This Year's Tax Rate	Last Year's Tax Paid	This Year's Tax Paid	$ This Year's Tax Paid (+) Change <->	% This Year's Tax Paid (+) Change <->
Land	16,000	18.6	20,000	20	+4,000	+25.0	.012	.012	192	240	+48	+25.0
Improvements	70,000	81.4	80,000	80	+10,000	+14.3	.012	.012	840	960	+120	+14.3
Total	86,000	100	100,000	100	+14,000	+16.3	.012	.012	1,032	1,200	+168	+16.3

Description	Last Year's Assessed Valuation	Last Year's %	This Year's Assessed Valuation	This Year's %	$ Valuation (+) Change <->	% Valuation (+) Change <->	Last Year's Tax Rate	This Year's Tax Rate	Last Year's Tax Paid	This Year's Tax Paid	$ This Year's Tax Paid (+) Change <->	% This Year's Tax Paid (+) Change <->
Land												
Improvements												
Total												

Description	Last Year's Assessed Valuation	Last Year's %	This Year's Assessed Valuation	This Year's %	$ Valuation (+) Change <->	% Valuation (+) Change <->	Last Year's Tax Rate	This Year's Tax Rate	Last Year's Tax Paid	This Year's Tax Paid	$ This Year's Tax Paid (+) Change <->	% This Year's Tax Paid (+) Change <->
Land												
Improvements												
Total												

FIGURE 8.4 Your Homeowner's Lifetime Property Assessment Tax Record

Example: _____
Last Year: _____ **This Year:** _____

Description	Last Year's Assessed Valuation	Last Year's %	This Year's Assessed Valuation	This Year's %	$ Valuation (+) Change <->	% Valuation (+) Change <->	Last Year's Tax Rate	This Year's Tax Rate	Last Year's Tax Paid	This Year's Tax Paid	$ This Year's Tax Paid (+) Change <->	% This Year's Tax Paid (+) Change <->
Land												
Improvements												
Total												

Description	Last Year's Assessed Valuation	Last Year's %	This Year's Assessed Valuation	This Year's %	$ Valuation (+) Change <->	% Valuation (+) Change <->	Last Year's Tax Rate	This Year's Tax Rate	Last Year's Tax Paid	This Year's Tax Paid	$ This Year's Tax Paid (+) Change <->	% This Year's Tax Paid (+) Change <->
Land												
Improvements												
Total												

Description	Last Year's Assessed Valuation	Last Year's %	This Year's Assessed Valuation	This Year's %	$ Valuation (+) Change <->	% Valuation (+) Change <->	Last Year's Tax Rate	This Year's Tax Rate	Last Year's Tax Paid	This Year's Tax Paid	$ This Year's Tax Paid (+) Change <->	% This Year's Tax Paid (+) Change <->
Land												
Improvements												
Total												

Q. *Is it really worth doing all of this if the amount I save on taxes is small, let's say $200 a year?*

A. The feeling of satisfaction that you are being taxed fairly may be worth all of your effort. Even a small savings can be satisfying. But no matter what the amount, you will have a reward in knowing that you at least helped yourself, you learned something in the process, and you can always seek a bigger reduction next time or for another house you move into later.

Q. *Can my property taxes be raised if I make a property tax appeal?*

A. In most states, it is illegal to raise the assessed value when an appeal has been filed. In effect, that would be penalizing you for exercising a right you have, which is to question your assessed value. So, proceed with enthusiasm and don't be concerned that an appeal will result in an increase. The exception is if the facts illustrate that an increase is in order. Your assessed value can then be raised. However, that won't happen if you properly analyze the data.

Useful Internet Resources

USING THE WORLD WIDE WEB FOR PROPERTY TAX RESEARCH

In Step 5 you were shown a seven-part process for researching your homeowners property tax appeal. To review, those steps were:

1. Identify comparable properties and gather information about them.
2. Identify your comparables on the tax list.
3. Locate your comparables on the tax maps.
4. Obtain a copy of your property record card from the assessor's office.
5. Obtain sales information about your comparables.
6. Take pictures of your properly and the three best comparables.
7. Prepare an analysis of your tax challenge research.

Depending on where you live, as many as the first five of those seven steps may be performed, at least in part, in the comfort of your own home by taking advantage of the remarkable resources of the World Wide Web.

PUBLIC INFORMATION WEB SITES

The governments of all 50 states have official Web sites that describe their agencies' functions. In many states, county and municipal governments have their own Web sites, too. If you happen to live in one of these areas, your local assessor's office may very well have its own official Web site. All assessor Web sites provide basic information: the name of the assessor, the office's address, and contact information (phone, fax, and e-mail). In most cases, the sites also outline the responsibilities and duties of the assessor's office, and many offer detailed guidance for, among other things, appealing your property tax assessment. There are even some assessor's Web sites (e.g., Bloomington Township in Illinois, San Diego County in California, and Kennebunk, Maine) that let you actually search electronic versions of public records or download the forms and documents required for your appeal. Although there is often a modest fee (payable by credit card), this is *really* an example of your tax dollars at work!

In addition to the official government sites, there are many private companies on the Internet that offer fee-based research of public records. You should be cautious about using such services, however. When researching your property tax appeal, it's usually best to do it yourself.

GETTING THERE FROM HERE

Although the prospect of connecting your home computer with a vast, global network of interconnected PCs, mainframes, and supercomputers may seem daunting, it's really a relatively simple exercise. All you have to do is tell your search engine (such as Excite or Yahoo!—accessed through a Web browser such as Microsoft's Internet Explorer or Netscape's Navigator) what you're looking for, click on the "search" or "go" or "get it" button, and you're there.

Because each search engine uses different search criteria (some look only at the titles of Web pages, others look for hidden HTML metatags that identify the files' subject matter, and others scan the entire content of all the pages available), your Web-based research results may vary depending on which search engine you use. The variance is illustrated in Figure A.1, which compares the number of sites found using five of the most popular Internet search engines in early July, 1998. (Keep in mind, however, that quantity does not necessarily equal quality, and you will most likely need only one site, not thousands.)

FIGURE A.1　Sites Found Using Various Search Engines

SEARCH TERM	SEARCH ENGINE				
Punctuation and delimiters (" " and +) were used exactly as shown below. . .	**AOL**	**Excite**	**Infoseek**	**Lycos**	**Yahoo (Alta Vista)**
"county assessor's office"	634	490	499	912	5 (5,066)
"assessor's office"	3,450	3,450	1,234	1,163	5 (5,066)
"property tax appeal"	91	91	553	2	0 (282)
+ "assessor's office" + "public records"	57	57	42	187	0 (155)
TOTAL	**4,232**	**4,088**	**2,328**	**2,264**	**10 (10,489)**

In conducting a search of such a specific topic as your local property tax assessments, the process is particularly easy. Because you can limit your search to a particular city, county, or township (or whatever political subdivision is appropriate), you are unlikely to have to sort through thousands of Web pages to find what you're looking for. Figure A.2 compares the same search as Figure A.1, except it is limited to Orange County. Note how this simple geographic limitation dramatically simplifies an Orange County resident's search.

A LOOK AT THE FUTURE

One of the most complete and useful property tax appeal sites in the country is maintained by the assessor's office of the town of Kennebunk, Maine (www.kennebunk.maine.org/documents.html). While this site is, obviously, of little use to anyone who is researching a property tax appeal outside of Kennebunk, its content demonstrates the Internet's potential as an extremely useful and efficient tool for property tax research. Figure A.3 reprints the text from the site's main page. All the data, forms, and statutory materials are available free of charge.

Few assessors will have sites as complete and comprehensive as this one. Most tend to resemble Figure A.4, which reproduces the complete text of the Oak Park, Illinois, township assessor's office. The majority of good

FIGURE A.2 Comparison of Sites Found in a County-Specific Search

SEARCH TERM	SEARCH ENGINE				
Punctuation and delimiters (" " and +) were used exactly as shown below . . .	**AOL**	**Excite**	**Infoseek**	**Lycos**	**Yahoo (Alta Vista)**
+ "county assessor's office" + "orange county"	8	8	11	0	0 (48)
+ "assessor's office" + "orange county"	18	18	18	6	0 (97)
+ "property tax appeal" + "orange county"	1	1	2	1	0 (8)
+ "assessor's office" + "public records"+ "orange county"	1	0	0	1	0 (8)
TOTAL	**28**	**27**	**31**	**8**	**0 (161)**

local assessor sites will, like this one, include basic information, answers to frequently asked questions, and contact information. Other sites contain essential contact information and a list of services, such as the site illustrated in Figure A.5. And some sites have even less information—basically only the name, address, and telephone number of the assessor.

Even when the information on your local assessor's site is minimal, the Internet adds to your thorough search of resources to support your property tax appeal.

OTHER INTERNET RESOURCE SITES

In addition to the official assessor's office sites, the Internet gives the savvy surfer access to a worldwide library of legal opinions, court cases, and professional advice and services.

Legal Opinions

Many law firms and individual attorneys have posted informational Web sites that explain, in varying degrees of detail, the rights and responsibilities of property taxpayers under the law, the process and procedures

FIGURE A.3   Kennebunk, Maine, Assessor's Web site, Text of Front Page

Welcome to the Assessor's Office section of the Town's Web site.

There is extensive information available here that should be of interest to citizens, real estate professionals, attorneys, appraisers, surveyors and others.

We've organized the Assessor's pages into four major sections. Near the bottom of this page are links to the four major sections. Those sections contain information and, in some cases, downloadable files containing valuable data in digital form.

The "Assessing Information" section contains general information about what the Assessor does, together with links to more specific information about the Assessor's Department and documents that cover the most common issues that arise. We have also made available an "APPLICATION FOR ABATEMENT OF PROPERTY TAXES" under Title 36 M.R.S.A. §841, that you may print out and use.

In the "Database" section we have included a complete database of tax records in "zip" format, updated as of the end of the previous quarter and available for download. The most recently available property sales figures for the town are now available and will be updated periodically as soon as we receive them from officials of the County of York. See the section for more information about the types of programs you'll need in order to view this information.

You will also find information about the town's Geographic Information System (GIS) and a complete collection of the town's GIS data in "zip" format for download. Please see the Software Requirements and TechNotes sections if you are unfamiliar with downloading or unzipping files.

Finally, in the Online Maps section we have made available all of the Town Tax Maps in two formats that allow them to be viewed online. These maps take advantage of ESRI's (Environmental Research Systems Institute) Internet ArcView Mapserver or a Netscape "plugin" that allow users to zoom in from a bird's eye view of the whole town down to an individual lot. Please be aware that most of the information is available in one format or another to users of all popular computer platforms. However, to take full advantage of all that we will have to offer, you should be using Netscape 3.0 or higher, Windows 95 or NT and have Java enabled. More information is available about software requirements along with some technical notes. Please read it before going much further.

Office Hours: Municipal Building Monday–Friday 8:30 AM–5 PM
(Please call 985-4852 or send email to request an appointment)
Address: 1 Summer Street
Kennebunk, Maine 04043
Phone: (207)985-4852
FAX: (207)985-4609
E-mail tm@cybertours.com

FIGURE A.4   Oak Park, Illinois, Township Assessor's Site

TAX AND ASSESSMENT NEWS

The process of real estate assessment and taxation is inherently complex, and there are unique aspects of the Cook County process. Accordingly, Township Assessor Galen L. Gockel answers many of the most asked questions below.

What determines the size of my tax bill? Property tax bills are the product of two main factors: 1) the Assessed Valuation placed on each individual home and 2) the tax rate of the community. Let's take each of them in turn.

Who places an Assessed Valuation on my home...and how is it done? Every three years the Cook County assessor makes a new attempt to estimate the value of all property in the County. Oak Park is in a section which was last reassessed in 1996, and we will all receive "Notices of Proposed Assessment" in 1999 . . . probably in the summer. The County uses actual, recent sales prices of comparable nearby homes to estimate the value of your home. If your new neighbors have paid top dollar for their homes, your Assessed Valuation will rise. Conversely if prices are stagnant in a community, its Assessed Valuations will not change.

What happens after the value of my home is estimated? By County ordinance, the Assessor is to assess at 16% of value for homes, condos, and rental structures containing six units or less. However our research indicates that the ratio of assessment to price actually averages about 10%.

What if we think the Assessed Valuation is too high? Complain to the County! But, you have to have a defensible case. Perhaps the County Assessor has exaggerated the size of your home. Or perhaps nearby comparable homes all have lower assessed valuations. We can help you develop and submit your complaint.

What about exemptions? If your home is occupied as a principal residence, the Homeowner's Exemption reduces your Equalized Assessed Valuation by $4,500. In addition, if you are a senior, regardless of income it comes down by an additional $2,500, but you must apply. For additional details, call us at the number below.

What determines Oak Park's tax rate? Most simply, the community-wide tax rate is determined by the spending levels of the 16 bodies which serve Oak Park. Over 63% of the most recent bill went to Elementary School District 97 and to OPRF High School; another 12% to Village Hall. Most recently, our 1996 tax rate (for taxes paid during 1997) was $12.537 per $100 of a home's Equalized Assessed Valuation. Tax rates vary from community to community, and from one year to the next.

FIGURE A.4 Oak Park, Illinois, Township Assessor's Site (Continued)

When do tax bills arrive? The first installment of our 1997 tax bills was mailed by the Cook County Collector in late January 1998 with a payment due date of March 1, 1998. Its amount was arbitrarily set at one-half of the previous year's total bill. Over the summer, community tax rates will be calculated, exemptions factored in, and the year's taxes will be calculated. Then, around August 1998, but maybe later, the second installment bill is mailed. It will be the difference between the year's taxes and the amount already paid on March 1. Consider a home whose bill last year was $4,000 and turns out to be $4,400 this year. The March 1, 1998 amount will be $2,000 and the August amount will be $2,400. If your taxes are being paid by your mortgage lender out of an escrow account, it will be billed electronically. If yours is a new loan, you might call your lender to make sure the tax bill has arrived there and is being paid.

What if I don't understand my tax bill, or think there is a mistake? Call us at 708-383-8005. We can interpret it for you or update its mailing name and address. If you did not receive your bill, we can obtain a duplicate from the County Collector.

Are there tax-relief programs for Senior Citizens? Yes, but they require the household income be below a certain level. The township can provide additional information.

Galen L. Gockel
Certified Illinois Assessing Officer
Township Assessor

Sally F. Nott
Certified Illinois Assessing Officer
Deputy Assessor

708-383-8005

for appealing an assessment, and analysis of the strengths and weaknesses of various arguments and strategies.

Obviously, the lawyers are not posting all this free information solely out of the goodness of their hearts or their abiding interest in a fully informed citizenry. They are hoping to build future business, or encourage you to consult with or retain them. Of course, there's nothing wrong with that; just be aware that your information resource may have an important motivation.

Another vital caveat: the Internet is a global resource, and laws (as well as assessment appeal procedures) vary significantly from one assessor's office to the next. Following advice that was successful in Bozeman may

---

FIGURE A.5   Essex, Vermont Assessor's Site

Town of Essex, Vermont U.S.A.
Assessor's Office

Location: 81 Main Street (2nd floor)

Phone Number: 878-1345

Hours:
7:30 AM – 4:30 PM
Monday through Friday

Staff Contact: Robert Barry, Assessor

Services:

- Appraisal and assessment of all taxable real estate, and personal property.
- Maintain property information records, sales information, and tax maps. Make information available to other departments, outside agencies, and to the general public.

Information Available:

May be researched by individuals desiring the information.

- Transfer information (deed book and page, sale date and price paid).
- Property ownership information, mailing addresses as of the most recent April 1st.
- Physical descriptions of taxable properties.

Records Available for Review:

- Property record folders.
- Tax maps.
- Work copies of recent Grand Lists.
- Transfer and ownership information.
- State orthophotos, 1978 and 1988 flights.
- Computerized maps.

Items Available for Sale:

- Copies of Assessor produced records, but not copies of other items, such as deeds, letters, maps, etc.

Cost of copies at Standard Town rate:

Street Maps $3.00
Tax maps (full size) $5.00
Mini tax maps $2.00

Notes: Copies of documents officially lodged with the Town Clerk, such as deeds, plats, the Official Grand List, etc., should be obtained from that office. Copies of proprietary materials should be obtained from the owner.

send your appeal down in flames in Savannah. Be sure that the legal information you're getting comes from a reliable, local source. Your state and local bar associations, for instance, may have useful information posted on their Web sites.

Court Cases and Public Records

The U.S. Supreme Court, federal courts, and most state courts have online databases of their decisions. While the decisions of the nation's highest courts probably will have little bearing on your local property tax appeal, the Internet also offers access to lower state court decisions, and many local government Web sites include archives of administrative decisions—such as property tax appeals (see Figure A.6 for two examples of potentially relevant decisions found on the Internet).

In addition, most states publish their statutes, as well as updates and new legislation, on the Internet. Many local governments also post their ordinances, codes, regulations, and minutes of council meetings. Figure A.7 shows how an Internet search for a pertinent Indiana statute would alert the property owner that a change in the law was pending.

Professional Advice

Finally, the Internet is a place where you can access all sorts of professional advice, which may be highly useful to you when researching your appeal. Accountants, tax consultants, and citizen activists often provide useful information. Of course, as with the attorneys' sites, approach any information provided free on the Internet with some reasonable suspicion. Before you take any advice seriously, and certainly before you act on it, be sure you know

- *who it's from.* Is the resource a reliable, respected source with a good reputation for integrity, thoroughness and accuracy? A university, for instance, might be a more reliable source of information than an anonymous personal home page.

FIGURE A.6   Examples of Relevant Legal Decisions Available on the Web

Case Name	Site Address	Issue	Decision
BFW Company, REALTOR®, vs. Office of Appellate Courts, County of Ramsey, Respondent: Supreme Court of Minnesota	http://www.finance-commerce.com/court/opinions/970718/bfw.htm	Minnesota Statute requires a taxpayer challenging a property tax assessment to provide county with all available information, even information the taxpayer deems incomplete or not fully accurate. This property tax appeal turns on question of what is the statutory obligation imposed on a petitioner to provide information to the county?	The plain meaning of the statute requires a petitioner to provide the county assessor with all information within its possession.
Oregon Tax Court Stanley E. and E. Kay Clark, *et al.* vs. Department of Revenue	http://www.ai.org/legislative/ic/code/title6/ar1.1/ch15.html	This appeal concerns the 1995-96 assessed value of property located in Deschutes County. Taxpayers claim the department erred by permitting the assessor to submit evidence at the administrative hearing of a value greater than the assessed value, and by relying on that evidence.	Statute only prohibits assessor from *changing* the tax roll. It does not prohibit an assessor in an appeal from changing his or her *valuation judgment.*

- *why they're providing the information.* What is the resource's motive in providing the information? Is it providing information solely as a public service or is there some possible political or (more likely) profit motive underlying the advice? For example, information from a tax protester site might be skewed to encourage you to act just to further the organization's political goals, regardless of the soundness of your case or the appropriateness of an appeal. We've already discussed the motive of law firms and lawyers, but accountants, consultants and other service providers should be listened to with some skepticism, too.

FIGURE A.7 Statutory Material on the Web

IC 6-1.1-15-1a

Note: This version of section effective until 1-1-99. See also following version of this section, effective 1-1-99.

Sec. 1. (a) A taxpayer may obtain a review by the county board of review of a county or township official's action with respect to the assessment of the taxpayer's tangible property if the official's action requires the giving of notice to the taxpayer. At the time that notice is given to the taxpayer, he shall also be informed in writing of:
   (1) his opportunity for review under this section; and
   (2) the procedures he must follow in order to obtain review under this section.

Source: Office of Code Revision, Indiana Legislative Services Agency
www.publications.ojd.state.or.us/TC4061.htm

- *what they want you to do for them.* Is the resource really after your money? Does it encourage you to sign up for a service, buy "quick-and-easy" software, attend a seminar or do anything else that involves parting with your paycheck? Remember, one of the main virtues of the Internet is that so much information—virtually infinite information—is available free to anyone who surfs by. When informational resources are really advertisers, take what you need and discard the "tainted" portion. Just be wary; don't let the Internet take advantage of you.

SURFER BEWARE!

Although we've already mentioned it a couple of times, it can't be said too often or too emphatically—don't let the amazing potential of the Internet as a research tool make you lazy! The process outlined in detail throughout this book is a sound, thorough, conservative strategy that, if followed, will help ensure that your appeal has its best chance of succeeding.

The Internet is only one weapon in your research arsenal, and for all its advantages, it is one that can easily backfire.

To ensure the most effective and accurate results from your Internet-assisted research, keep the following points in mind:

- *Trust no one.* One of the big attractions of the Internet for some is its anonymity—no one knows who you really are. Internet users sometimes abuse this feature by adopting false "Internet identities." Just because someone has a Web site, it doesn't mean they are offering accurate, useful, or even legally sound advice or information. Be a suspicious consumer of Internet services.
- *Be sure of your sources, be careful of your facts.* As with any deal, if someone on the Internet promises something that seems too good to be true, it probably is.
- *Ask questions.* Don't be afraid to ask for help, and don't hesitate to consult a competent attorney if you have questions.
- *Don't assume you can do it all from home.* Some research must be performed, and some documents obtained, only in person. Know the procedural and documentation rules for pursuing an appeal, and follow them to the letter. If the Internet can help you find facts, figures, and other information more quickly and easily, great. If you use the Internet to cut corners, your appeal's chances of success may suffer. The Internet is a valuable tool, but it's just a tool. And like any other kind of tool, if you don't use it properly and with caution, you may get hurt. That's why you need to know the steps discussed throughout this book. Understanding the old-fashioned way will ensure that you use your high-tech tool effectively.

A BRAVE NEW WORLD, OR NOT

In 20 years, the days of homeowners laboriously paging through public records in the assessor's office to prepare their property tax appeals may be the stuff of picturesque historical anecdotes. Today, we are in a transitional period, and no one can accurately predict where we'll end up. As we've seen, the Internet offers enormous potential for helping you perform the kind of research and preparation necessary for a successful property tax appeal. As we've also seen, however, the quality of information and services available vary wildly from one jurisdiction to the next. If you're lucky enough to live in a town like Kennebunk, Maine, you'll have vital information, forms, and services at your fingertips. If you live in a town that doesn't even have a Web site, you've got your work cut out for you.

One very useful resource for homeowners to use is the database that is being developed by a joint effort by the Appraisal Institute, the largest American appraisal society, and FNC, Inc., an Internet software firm.

The database will contain detailed appraisal information on the World Wide Web that will be available to homebuyers, homesellers, REALTORS®, mortgage lenders, Wall Street investors, marketing firms, and anyone else with interests in real estate.

Currently, home value estimate data on the Internet is based primarily on publicly recorded sales prices and market trend analyses. The new venture will integrate appraiser's property files with the Internet via interface technology created by FNC, Inc.

This system will be operational sometime in 1999. It will allow users to check out homes and entire neighborhoods anywhere in the country for between $5 and $10 per property.

Data will be taken from the Uniform Residential Appraisal Report, which is currently used by appraisers nationwide to value a home. The information will include the following:

- A legal description of the house
- Current tax assessment data
- The sale price
- Price ranges of single-family homes
- Information about whether the homes are owner-occupied or rentals
- The types of commercial or other land uses in the neighborhood
- Market trend patterns
- Real estate listings and sales

- Square footage of the lot and living space
- Topography of the lot
- Utilities information
- Age
- Architectural style
- Type of foundation
- Roof
- Windows
- Basement
- Drainage
- Number of rooms and layout
- Kitchen equipment
- Heating and air-conditioning systems
- Insulation
- General evaluation of the condition of each of the features above

To use this system, users will enter search criteria, such as price range, number of bedrooms, neighborhood, etc., and will receive comparable residential sales and prices from the database. Consumers will pay for this information with a credit card. High-volume users, such as real estate companies and mortgage companies, will be billed by formal contract.

This new service should be particularly helpful to families moving from one part of the country to another. They will be able to search the Web, get an idea of what their current house is worth, and get a feeling for prevailing values in the neighborhoods they want to live in.

Examples of Successful Property Tax Appeals

SITUATION 1:
HOMEOWNER'S PROPERTY TAX APPEALS

To be sure that you thoroughly understand what must be done to prepare a successful appeal, let's examine the property tax situation of John and Mary Doe. They are typical homeowners who live in Middletown, USA. They think their property taxes are too high, but they know that in order to get a reduction they will have to prove to the local tax authorities that their property is valued too high. So they decide to gather the appropriate information and prepare an appeal. Here is what they did.

John and Mary live in a development of about 125 homes that range in market value between $159,000 and $193,000. About six months ago, they considered selling their house, but decided to remain there for another few years. At that time, they asked a REALTOR® to prepare a market analysis to establish a fair market price for their home. (Keep in mind that a market analysis by a real estate salesperson, or an appraisal by an independent appraiser, employs comparables to estimate the approximate value of a property.) The results of the REALTOR®'s analysis indicated that a price of $183,000 would be about right for their property. Not much has changed in the real estate marketplace since this analysis. Their house was valued by the assessor at $192,500.

John and Mary know of a house on the next block that sold for $182,000 about two months ago. The taxes on that property are $1,255 per year. The house is similar to theirs—a ranch with a full basement, three bedrooms, one and a half baths, 1,600 square feet of living space, and a double garage. The tax on John and Mary's property is $1,685 per year.

John and Mary don't understand why they are paying so much more in taxes, but they plan to find out by doing a market analysis and by examining the records for their property in the Middletown tax assessor's office.

Single Family House

John began by driving around the neighborhood to locate some comparable properties. When identifying them, he kept in mind that they should be in close proximity to his property, usually within one to two miles, of similar style, age, and size, and sold within the last year or during the assessment tax period, depending on state law.

He found six houses he thought would meet these criteria and wrote a brief description of each one.

- *Comparable #1:* 3BR ranch, 1-car attached garage, fenced yard, wood siding, asphalt roof, paved driveway, small deck in back. Address: 86 Mill Ave.
- *Comparable #2:* 3BR ranch, 1-car attached garage, brick construction, asphalt roof, paved driveway, air conditioning. Address: 107 Hemlock.
- *Comparable #3:* 3BR ranch, 1-car attached garage, aluminum siding, asphalt-shingle roof, cement driveway, fireplace. Address: 156 Hemlock.
- *Comparable #4:* 3BR ranch, 1-car attached garage, wood siding, stone driveway, nice landscaping, window air conditioner, asphalt roof. Address: 4 Maple Ave.
- *Comparable #5:* 3BR ranch, 1-car attached garage, paved driveway, aluminum siding, fenced yard in back, storage shed, fireplace, deck. Address: 217 Furnace Road.
- *Comparable #6:* 3BR ranch, wood siding with stone facing in front, fireplace, pool, paved driveway, asphalt roof, air conditioning. Address: 147 Palmer Terrace.

John gave this information to Mary, and she went to the Middletown assessor's office to gather more data. She located each of the properties on a tax list and then on a tax map. She obtained the lot and block numbers, confirmed the addresses and owners' names, the assessed values, the annual taxes, and the property classifications, and she drew a sketch of each lot that included the dimensions.

Mary also searched for information about the sale of each of these properties. One of them, the house located at 147 Palmer Terrace, had been sold more than three years ago. The house at 107 Hemlock had not been sold as John thought.

Mary asked the assessor for a copy of her property record card. The assessor furnished it without any resistance. When she asked for the cards on the other properties, she was told that she could look at them, but couldn't have a copy. She took notes about the assessments, the size of the improvements, the number of bedrooms and bathrooms, basements, etc.

When Mary got home, she and John reviewed the information that she had gathered. When Mary mentioned that one of the houses had not been sold and that another was sold more than three years ago, John decided to look for other comparables to replace them. He remembered a house that was two miles away in another development that was sold a year ago. He drove over to see it and wrote a description. The house had four bedrooms, a fireplace, air conditioning, a paved driveway, and about 2,000 square feet of living area, and was located on a corner lot.

Next, John and Mary filled out a market data analysis form and completed an equity analysis as well. They decided that the last house that John researched was too far away and was substantially larger than theirs and the others. They felt the others would be better comparables.

Mary contacted her REALTOR® and asked for some help with the cost-adjustment factors. She introduced Mary to an appraiser with whom she does business. The appraiser helped Mary find the data that she needed to complete the market analysis and check the property record card calculations (computations and adjustments for the type of construction, the pavement on the driveway, the deck, plumbing, electrical, etc.). [Note: If you don't know any REALTORS®, you can get adjustment figures from a tax assessor, an appraiser, or the library. Usually, REALTORS® are helpful because they are hoping for a listing and/or subsequent sale, or a reference for being helpful.] Mary also went back to the assessor's office and reviewed the state manual to learn more about the cost figures that were used on the record card. Once she had checked a few of the figures on the card against the state manual, she felt more confident. Mary found that she was able to properly verify the sources of the factors used and the accuracy of the assessor's computations.

Mary and John used this information for their discussion with the assessor. Both forms show an indicated value by market data analysis with comments, and a value per square foot. These figures are used to demonstrate the value that Mary and John believe should be established for their property. The adjustments demonstrate how and why the concluded value was derived. All of these data are used to persuade the tax assessor to change the value.

John and Mary prepared a brief outline of what they wanted to review with the assessor. They scheduled a meeting and went over the facts. Because they had taken the time and made the effort to analyze the data properly, they were successful in reducing their taxes to $1,305 per year. That's a savings of $380 each year. Their time was well spent!

Questions You Might Ask about This Case

- *Were the results of the market analysis done by the REALTOR® important in this appeal?* Not really. The potential sales price, although derived by the REALTOR® using comparables, is significant only as another opinion of value. It was an estimate of the price at which to list the property. It may not sell at that price. If you can demonstrate a lower market value with other valid sold comparables, you should use them. Be prepared, however, to defend your selection of comparables.

- *What significance did the house that sold for $182,000 have in this case?* It got the Does thinking about comparable properties and that a house similar to theirs was being taxed less than their home. This is the value of doing an equity analysis.

- *Why should the Does reject the additional comparable found by John in favor of the others?* It was larger by 25 percent. It was two miles away in a different development. By using comparables that are closer and in their own development, they were able to present a stronger case. The proximity of the comparables to your residence is very important in establishing value.

- *Why do an equity analysis when market value is the best approach to value?* An equity analysis, in those states that allow its use, is a good indication that a property is being overtaxed. It breaks down value on a square-footage basis for ease of comparison. If the comparables used are the same as those used in the market analysis—and they should be—your case is substantially strengthened because you are demonstrating in two ways that your residence is overtaxed.

- *Why is it important to check out the computations and factors used by the assessor on the property record card?* Cost is a recognized approach to value. If the figures used to assess your property yield a result that shows you should be taxed less, it may be the best approach to use in your case. Errors in computation or in the selection of adjustment factors can save you lots of money.

SITUATION 2:
A CASE OF DRAMATIC MATHEMATICAL ERROR

Joe Wilson, the mayor of a small town in Nevada, decided one day to take a look at the assessed value of his home. It seemed to him that the value was awfully high for a house its size. Joe went down to the assessor's office. He knew the assessor and was a bit hesitant, but he did it anyway. Joe was convinced something was wrong. His neighbor was paying about half the property taxes he was. It didn't seem fair to Joe.

Before visiting the assessor's office, Joe had measured the outside of his house and recorded the dimensions on a sheet of paper. He even made a small drawing of the house. The two-story house was an irregular shape.

It also had a basement the same size as the first floor that was finished with two bedrooms and a full bathroom.

Joe went to the assessor's office, politely greeted the assessor as he passed by his office, and proceeded to the main desk where he requested a copy of his property record card. When the clerk brought it, Joe noticed some interesting things. First, the picture of the house was very old. Although Joe hadn't made any additions, there wasn't much landscaping in the photograph and the storage shed in the backyard wasn't in the picture.

Joe asked for a copy of the card and went home to analyze it more completely and compare the measurements to the ones he had taken. Was he ever surprised when he started looking!

Joe had been careful to measure the outside walls of his house—which is how it should be done. He compared these measurements to the ones on the card. He noticed that the measurements of the rear of the house didn't equal the measurement of the front of the house. In fact, they were off by 33 feet. The measurements on the card were higher figures by an astounding amount. That meant he was being assessed for a much larger house. He continued looking, because he found this exciting.

Joe knew the basement and the first floor were the same size, but in the drawing on the card they were different. The basement dimensions shown were 10 feet smaller than the first floor measurements. And the first floor measurements differed from his measurements by more than 20 feet at one end of the house. He couldn't believe his eyes. He rechecked the figures. Sure enough, he was right. The basement was smaller and the first floor was larger. Joe started thinking he might have a good case.

The second floor has a lot of angles to it, so it took more time to check out the figures. But when Joe was done, he found it was time well spent. By his calculations, the second floor's square footage differed from the assessor's measurements by almost 300 square feet. That was a significant difference. Joe figured that the house hadn't been measured by the assessor for many years. Otherwise this discrepancy would have been found.

When Joe finished calculating, he found a total difference in square footage between the assessor's record and his measurements of more than

700 square feet—and the error was in his favor. Whew, what a nice day Joe was having.

Because of what he already found, he figured there must be other errors. He continued checking all the calculations on the card, such as the amount of asphalt shown for the driveway, and the measurements for the storage shed, which had been included in the square footage of the house by accident. What a mess, he thought!

For the past nine years, Joe had been paying for an additional 700 square feet of living area that didn't exist. He wondered if he could recoup that loss. Joe called an attorney friend who dealt in these matters. He discovered, however, that he could only recover the past two years of overpayment. The other taxes he already paid were lost forever. Joe wished he had done this sooner.

He assembled his data, called the assessor, and set up an appointment to talk. He summarized in detail all the figures he had assembled and prepared a chart showing the differences. He then calculated how much these differences amounted to in terms of assessed value. It turned out that he was overassessed $52,000 on which he was paying taxes. When his assessment was adjusted, it converted to a tax savings of over $600 per year. That's a loss of $4,200 for the seven years he cannot recover. Joe was sick about that, but he was able to get a reduction in assessed value. And he recovered $1,200 in overpayments for the past two years. The most important thing Joe did, though, was to tell the assessor the assessed value he thought should be on his home. He didn't leave it up to the assessor.

Joe was very polite and noncritical when he talked to the assessor. They parted as friends and ultimately Joe was a whole lot richer than before. It took a couple of months before the reduction was final, but it was worth his effort. Plus, each year from now on, he will save at least $600.

Questions You Might Ask about This Case

- *Why couldn't Joe collect for the other seven years?* In most states, the law only allows you to recover the past year in taxes. In Joe's case, the law was two years.

- *Could Joe have appealed higher and recovered the overpayment for those seven years?* No, most laws clearly state the limit of retroactive recovery of overpayments. So Joe was out of luck on this count.
- *Why did Joe tell the assessor what he thought the assessed value should be?* The answer is simple. If he hadn't, the assessor would have been more likely to settle for a higher amount. By asking for what he felt was right, Joe was successful in getting all he was entitled to, not just a part of it. The assessor could have easily decided on a higher assessed value and Joe would have had to appeal his case to a higher level. He wanted to avoid that if possible. His strategy paid off.
- *Why did Joe check all the other calculations after he already found a significant reduction?* There are so many factors that affect the assessed value that Joe felt it was worth the time to check everything. He was right. Even if he didn't find any other errors, he would feel satisfied that his record was correct and his taxes were fair and equitable. He achieved peace of mind by checking further.

SITUATION 3: KNOW WHAT YOU'RE DOING

Don Smith just got his tax bill and couldn't believe how much his taxes had gone up. He was really angry and wanted to do something about it but didn't know how. Don decided to go to the assessor's office and complain. He was certain there was some mistake.

The next day, he got in his car and drove there, hoping that a gross error had been made. When he arrived, he asked to speak to someone who could help him. A young man in his mid-30s appeared, and Don told him there had to be a mistake here. He hadn't added anything to his house for years, and it wasn't in good shape because he had been ill and didn't have the time or resources to make needed repairs. He explained how his neighbors all had nice houses, and he was being taxed as much as they were.

The young man—let's call him Ray—began explaining how the tax system worked. Don listened but still felt he was being overtaxed. Ray explained how budgets were set and how values in the area had gone up during the year. Don interrupted him and repeated that his house was not in good shape and the taxes were too high. Ray continued by showing Don how the assessed value had been calculated on his house. He said they used a system called "mass appraising." Don didn't understand what that was and kept telling Ray that his taxes weren't fair.

Ray told Don to appeal the assessment if he wanted to, but it looked fair to him. He said he couldn't do anything unless he had a formal protest. He handed Don a form and suggested that he fill it out and return it by the end of May, which was the end of the filing period in the state. Don had three weeks to complete the form.

Don went home, still grumbling to himself about the high taxes on his house. When he got home, he looked at the form and it called for information on three "comparable" homes like his. Don wasn't sure what a comparable was, so he asked his neighbor, Joe. Joe told Don that comparables had to be two-story houses like his. Don wondered where he would get them. He thought of his daughter's friend who had just started in real estate sales six months ago. So, Don called him.

When Bill answered the phone at the real estate office, Don told him that he needed information on comparable sales to fill out his protest form. Bill had never done a tax protest, but said he would get him sales data because he knew how to do that.

Two days later, Bill called Don and supplied him with the sales data on three comparable two-story homes in his area. Don thanked him and asked Bill to fax them to his office.

Don went to his office that afternoon and looked at the data. He compared it with what was on the form. It called for the sale date, style of house, square footage, and several other items. He transferred the data from the sold listings Bill had supplied. He was still angry and felt he was being cheated by the government. Bill had selected good comparables because each of the properties was being taxed less than his was and should show those government guys how wrong they were. He thought more about the needed repairs on his house and that the other homes in the neighborhood were in good shape. Don noted that in the remarks section and thought he had filled out the form fairly well. He placed the completed form in an envelope, put a stamp on, and mailed it the next day. It was still a week before the deadline, so he thought it would get there in plenty of time.

A few days later, Don called Ray in the assessor's office to ask if he had received the envelope. Ray told him he hadn't, but that the clerk would see it before he did and not to worry. It was several days before the deadline, and Ray was sure that if it hadn't already arrived, it would be there on time.

That made Don feel better, and he didn't think about it for a week. When called again, Ray said it had arrived a day late. Their policy was to reject any appeals that arrived after the deadline date. Don didn't like that and told Ray in no uncertain terms that he mailed it in time and expected him to review the appeal anyway. Don was angry and it was obvious. Ray said he would have to check with his supervisor. Don again told Ray that it had been mailed on time, and he saw no reason why his appeal couldn't be processed.

The next morning, Ray called and said that his supervisor was hesitant to review the appeal because it arrived late, but that since Don claimed he had mailed it on time and it was only a day late, he would allow Ray to proceed with the review. Don was satisfied for the moment.

About a week later, Ray called Don and told him the comparable sales he had selected were sold during the past six months, in fact one of them in the past month. He explained that he had no choice but to deny the appeal and explained that the sales had to have occurred during a certain period. Did Don know that or had he read it on the form? Ray asked. Don said he hadn't noticed it, but that surely his daughter's friend knew what he was doing. Ray politely told him that he had to deny the appeal.

Naturally, Don was furious. He threatened to talk to Ray's supervisor. Ray was very polite and said he was free to do that, and he was sorry that he had to deny the protest.

That afternoon, Don called Ray's supervisor, and she repeated what Ray had told him and said she was sorry, but those were the rules. She tried to calm Don down and was polite and understanding. Now he would have to wait until next year to refile his protest. The worst part, though, was that he had to pay the higher taxes for a whole year, and he knew that wasn't fair.

Questions You Might Ask about This Case

- *What's wrong with mailing in the protest form?* Usually, there isn't anything wrong with mailing in the form, unless you are close to the deadline. There is always a possibility the mail could be delayed, which could be costly, as it was in this situation. A better alternative would be to take the appeal form to the assessor's office and get a receipt that shows you filed it.

- *What potential impact did Don's behavior at the assessor's office have on getting a favorable decision in his case?* Don was angry during his discussions with Ray. Even though he was upset, he should have been polite. Very likely Ray wasn't the person who calculated the assessed value for Don's house. Why take it out on Ray? Don's behavior could have made Ray angry, too, and he could have suggested to his supervisor that the appeal be denied. Fortunately for Don, Ray didn't react that way. Even if Don had a strong protest with valid reasons and great comparables, he could have lost his case without ever having had a chance to be heard.

- *Why are current sales as comparables not allowed?* The answer is simple. In each state, a cutoff date for comparable sales is established by law. If you don't follow the rules, you lose. In Don's case, he lost big.

SITUATION 4: IS THE REDUCTION YOU'RE ASKING FOR LARGE ENOUGH?

George and Penny live in an average neighborhood in their area. Homes are priced in the range of $120,000 to $160,000. The property taxes on most homes in their subdivision are in the range of $960 to $1,280 per year. Unfortunately, George and Penny are being taxed at the high end of that range—about $1,240. They talked from time to time about how their taxes seemed high for the size of their house compared to others in the subdivision. They thought a fairer tax would be $1,160 per year. And, they felt their assessed value, the amount on which their taxes would be calculated, should be about $145,000 and not the current assessed value of $155,000.

George and Penny knew something about how to file a tax protest. They had done it successfully eight years before; they were confident they would be successful this time. They began gathering the appropriate information for their appeal and organized it for their presentation. Then they wrote a letter to the assessor, attached the data they had gathered, and took it to his office. The facts they had put together indicated a reduction of $10,000 in the assessed value of their home, which seemed reasonable to them.

A couple of weeks after the deadline expired, George got a notice to appear at a hearing for his appeal, at which time they would be able to present the facts he and Penny had put together. The data they had compiled indicated that they would save about $80 a year in taxes. That wasn't much, but they thought their tax should be fair; it was more the principle of the matter than anything else.

George and Penny went to the hearing, presented their case well, and went home to await a reply from the assessor's office. The reply came about two weeks later. The letter indicated their appeal had been denied. After thinking it over, they decided not to appeal further.

Questions You Might Ask about This Case

- *Why was their appeal denied?* In this case, the amount of tax reduction was $80 or about 6 percent. Although that is small, it is a reduction nevertheless and money in the pockets of George and Penny. And, they were appealing on the principle that they were being unfairly taxed. The facts probably supported that view.

- *Why didn't they win a reduction?* In all likelihood, the county assessor's office decided that the amount of administrative costs incurred to issue a refund and process a tax reduction was too high, and the amount of reduction was too small to be worth their further time in the matter. The percentage change was small, as well.

The point is that it may not be worth your while to file a protest appeal that results in less than an 8 percent or 10 percent reduction. The reason is that administration costs may be higher than the reduction, and the government would have to make up the deficit to pay for administrative costs of running the property tax system in the county. Secondly, the estimated values of properties are an opinion, not a science. When George and Penny decided their property was worth $145,000, they may have been right, but there is a margin of error. Even in an appraisal done by a professional, the estimated value is an opinion. Another appraiser valuing the same house could come up with a different value rather easily.

The bottom line: Make it worth your time to prepare and present your case and the county's time to hear your appeal.

Blank Forms

This checklist and these forms have been provided for your use in preparing for your winning property tax appeal. Please feel free to make copies of them for that purpose.

REASONS TO CHALLENGE YOUR HOMEOWNER'S PROPERTY TAX

Check all that apply to your assessment.

☐ Assessed at more than legal percentage
☐ Improper classification of property
☐ Assessment higher than state-issued sales assessment ratio
☐ Assessor used wrong approach in valuation according to state manual
☐ Property assessed in wrong class
☐ Property listed in wrong assessment district
☐ Income valuation used in error
☐ Exemptions for property use not recognized
☐ Exempt personal property included in homeowner's assessment
☐ Personal exemptions not granted or applied
☐ No notice of increased assessment was issued or received
☐ Maintenance items used to increase assessment

☐ Standard cost manual improperly used
☐ Wrong property assessed
☐ Property assessed at more than market value
☐ Assessments on similar properties are lower
☐ Property recently purchased for less than assessed value
☐ Assessment higher than construction costs
☐ Environmental restrictions not considered
☐ Easement restrictions not considered
☐ Property not inspected
☐ Important information omitted from record card
☐ Record is out of date
☐ Mechanical, clerical, computational, or mathematical errors
☐ Depreciation allowances made in error
☐ Failure to note depreciation of on-site conditions
☐ Failure to note depreciation of off-site conditions
☐ Grade and quality of improvements wrong
☐ Shoddy construction not noted
☐ Lack of utilities not noted
☐ Age of home listed incorrectly
☐ Description of land incorrect
☐ Dimensions of land incorrect
☐ Overall description incorrect
☐ Description of buildings incorrect
☐ Dimensions of improvements incorrect
☐ Dimensions of building incorrect
☐ Finished areas are listed incorrectly

RESIDENTIAL MARKET DATA ANALYSIS

Subject Property

Legal Description:

_____

_____

_____

_____

_____

_____

_____

PASTE UP PHOTO OF YOUR HOME

Assessor's Property
Identification #:

_____

_____

_____

_____

	Subject	Comp. #1		Comp. #2		Comp. #3	
Property Address							
Distance to Subj.							
Sales Price	$	$		$		$	
Price/Liv. Area S/F	$	$		$		$	
Source of Data							
	Description	**Description**	**Adj. ±**	**Description**	**Adj. ±**	**Description**	**Adj. ±**
Date of Sale and Adjustment/Time							
Living Area S/F							
Location							
Site/View							
Design and Appeal							
Quality/Constr.							
Age							
Condition							
Room Count							
Total							
Bedrooms							
Baths							
Basement							
Finished							
Unfinished							
Garage/Carport							
Porch/Patio							
Other							
Swimming Pool							
Fireplace							
Kitchen Equip.							
Remodeling							
Air-conditioning							
Net Adj.—Total			±		±		±
Indicated Value	$	$		$		$	

Comments: _____

_____

Indicated Value by Market Data Analysis _____ $ _____

or $ _____ per S/F

RESIDENTIAL EQUITY ANALYSIS
Subject Property

Legal Description:

_____

_____

_____

_____

_____

_____

_____

PASTE UP PHOTO OF YOUR HOME

Assessor's Property
Identification #:

_____

_____

_____

_____

	Subject	Comp. #1		Comp. #2		Comp. #3	
Property Address							
Distance to Subj.							
Sales Price	$	$		$		$	
Price/Liv. Area S/F	$	$		$		$	
Source of Data							
	Description	Description	Adj. ±	Description	Adj. ±	Description	Adj. ±
Date of Sale and Adjustment/Time							
Living Area S/F							
Location							
Site/View							
Design and Appeal							
Quality/Constr.							
Age							
Condition							
Room Count							
Total							
Bedrooms							
Baths							
Basement							
Finished							
Unfinished							
Garage/Carport							
Porch/Patio							
Other							
Swimming Pool							
Fireplace							
Kitchen Equip.							
Remodeling							
Air-conditioning			±		±		±
Net Adj.—Total							
Indicated Value	$	$		$		$	

Indicated Value by Equity Analysis $_____

or $ _____ per S/F

Comments: _____

_____

_____

How Much Will You Save?

This Year's Tax Assessment	Select One	Projected % Cut	=	Projected $ Cut	Select One	# of Years	=	Projected Tax Savings
	X	1	=		X	1	=	
	X	2	=		X	2	=	
	X	3	=		X	3	=	
	X	4	=		X	4	=	
	X	5	=		X	5	=	
	X	6	=		X	6	=	
	X	7	=		X	7	=	
	X	8	=		X	8	=	
	X	9	=		X	9	=	
	X	10	=		X	10	=	
	X	11	=		X	11	=	
	X	12	=		X	12	=	
	X	13	=		X	13	=	
	X	14	=		X	14	=	
	X	15	=		X	15	=	
	X	16	=		X	16	=	
	X	17	=		X	17	=	
	X	18	=		X	18	=	
	X	19	=		X	19	=	
	X	20	=		X	20	=	
	X	21	=		X	21	=	
	X	22	=		X	22	=	
	X	23	=		X	23	=	
	X	24	=		X	24	=	
	X	25	=		X	25	=	
						30	=	

Example:_____
Last Year:_____ **This Year:**_____

Description	Last Year's Assessed Valuation	Last Year's %	This Year's Assessed Valuation	This Year's %	$ Valuation (+) Change <->	% Valuation (+) Change <->	Last Year's Tax Rate	This Year's Tax Rate	Last Year's Tax Paid	This Year's Tax Paid	$ This Year's Tax Paid (+) Change <->	% This Year's Tax Paid (+) Change <->
Land												
Improvements												
Total												

Description	Last Year's Assessed Valuation	Last Year's %	This Year's Assessed Valuation	This Year's %	$ Valuation (+) Change <->	% Valuation (+) Change <->	Last Year's Tax Rate	This Year's Tax Rate	Last Year's Tax Paid	This Year's Tax Paid	$ This Year's Tax Paid (+) Change <->	% This Year's Tax Paid (+) Change <->
Land												
Improvements												
Total												

Description	Last Year's Assessed Valuation	Last Year's %	This Year's Assessed Valuation	This Year's %	$ Valuation (+) Change <->	% Valuation (+) Change <->	Last Year's Tax Rate	This Year's Tax Rate	Last Year's Tax Paid	This Year's Tax Paid	$ This Year's Tax Paid (+) Change <->	% This Year's Tax Paid (+) Change <->
Land												
Improvements												
Total												

Glossary

acre A unit of measure for land consisting of 43,560 square feet.

adjustments Values used by assessors and appraisers to compensate for the differences between the subject property and comparables. For example, if the subject had two full bathrooms, but a comparable had three full bathrooms, a value would be attached to represent the difference of one full bathroom. The comparable would be adjusted downward in this case to make it more equal in value (more realistically comparable) to the subject property, as if the comparable had two bathrooms.

amenities Items existing on a site that may contribute to its overall value, such as a fence, a sprinkler system, or air conditioning.

appraised value The value of a property as determined by research and comparative data gathered by a real estate appraiser. It represents an opinion or estimate of a property's value.

approaches to value There are three methods used to determine the value of a residential property:

1. *Market data approach*—actual sales price paid for property, also known as the sales comparison approach.
2. *Cost approach*—the cost to replace or reproduce a structure (e.g., a house) using standard cost data supplied by a cost research firm.
3. *Equity approach*—a comparison of the assessed values on a square footage basis. This approach is accepted in only a few states.

Whenever possible, all approaches should be used to determine the value of a property for tax purposes. Because property values tend to change slowly, values derived using only one method may not reflect the actual property value. Abnormal market conditions of short duration may bring about prices that do not really indicate the true value of a property. Likewise, abnormal construction costs may also cause a distortion of the true value.

There is one other generally accepted method used to value properties. It is the income approach. It is used for both residential and commercial/industrial properties. However, in the residential arena, it is used only for investment properties, such as duplexes or apartment buildings. In preparing a property tax appeal for your home, you will not use this method.

assessed value An estimate of the value of a property in the opinion of the tax assessor. The value determined may be based on full market value or a fraction thereof. The assessed value is used to calculate the amount of tax due on a property.

assessment period The specific period of time during which your residence is valuated. For example, July 1st through June 30th of a certain year.

assessment ratio The ratio of assessed value to full market value. For example, assume a property sold for $80,000. If the assessed value is $40,000, the assessment ratio can be calculated by dividing the assessed value ($40,000) by the sale price ($80,000). The resulting ratio is 50 percent. An assessment ratio of 50 percent indicates that properties in the taxing municipality have an assessed value that is one-half (50%) of full market value.

The ratio may be defined either by statute (law) or by the relationship between assessed value and market value as determined by studies done by the taxing authorities.

block and lot A method of identifying a site by which lots are numbered within a block to separately identify them. A lot may be any size; there is no standard length or width. The block number is an arbitrary number assigned to identify a grouping of lots.

clerk and recorder's office A government office in which public records are kept for reference purposes for anyone who needs the information. Copies of deeds and liens on properties can be found in this office.

comparables Properties that have been sold that are used for comparison purposes in the assessment and appraisal processes. Comparables should be as similar as possible to the subject to which they are being compared in location (the same subdivision if possible), size (within 10 percent of the subject's square foot area, but not exceeding 20 percent), style (e.g., a ranch, a two-story, a bi-level), amenities (built-in dishwasher, deck, patio, sprinkler system), and year of construction.

contingency fees A fee charged by a property tax agent or an attorney who specializes in appealing the assessed value of properties. It is contingent on (depends on) a reduction in the value being achieved. If a reduction in the value is not attained, then nothing is owed.

contributory value The value of an amenity or component that contributes toward the overall value of improvements on a site. This value is usually less than the current cost of replacing the amenity and is used to make adjustments to the estimated value to derive the final estimated value of a comparable property.

depreciation The loss in value of any structure due to physical depreciation, functional obsolescence (loss over and above physical depreciation caused by factors within the subject property), or economic obsolescence (like functional obsolescence, but outside the subject property). Depreciation only applies to improvements, not land.

easement A right to use a portion of land for a specific or general purpose. For example, the right of a utility company to erect and maintain lines across a property. Or the right of a trucking company to cross the land to perform certain work on an adjoining property, such as transporting granite from a quarry.

flood map A map showing the classification of a site in terms of its flood risk and its location in or out of a flood zone.

full market value The sale price that would probably be arrived at through fair negotiations between a willing seller and a willing buyer, taking into consideration the uses to which the property may be put.

highest and best use The purpose for which a site and its improvements are used. For example, a residence may be the highest and best use of a site due to its location within an existing subdivision. On the other hand, a commercial mine may be the highest and best use for a property rich in precious gold.

market value A value determined by comparing a subject property to other similar properties that have been sold during an assessment period or within the past six months.

personal exemptions An exemption on your property taxes due to your personal class (e.g., widow, veteran, senior citizen). Some states have no personal exemptions.

plat map A map showing the dimensions of a site (the land on which a residence is constructed). These dimensions are the result of a survey made of the site. The map also indicates the relative location of the site, such as its lot and block number and street.

property identification number (P.I.N.) A unique number assigned by a local unit of government to identify a site.

property record card The assessor's worksheet for recording information about a residence. It often includes a structural drawing with measurements of the improvements, cost data, information about plumbing and electrical systems, assessed value, market value and other factors used to determine a property's assessed value for tax purposes.

record errors Computational or factual errors found on the property record card located in the tax assessor's office.

residential equity analysis approach A method of valuing a property for tax appeal purposes that shows the difference in assessed values and taxes for comparable properties. It is allowed in only a few states, but may be used to support your residential market data analysis.

residential market data analysis approach A method of valuing a property for tax appeal purposes that shows how comparable properties have a lower assessed value (and market value) than the subject property.

square footage A measurement derived by multiplying the outside length of one wall by the adjoining wall (e.g., a rectangular home measuring 40 feet by 30 feet would have 1,200 square feet of living area).

tax assessor The government official responsible for establishing the value of property for ad valorem tax purposes (a tax based solely upon value). He or she may be elected, appointed, or under civil service and may be known by many different names, such as evaluator, assessment commissioner, appraiser, or assessor. The assessor is responsible for discovering, listing, and valuing all taxable real and personal property within a taxing jurisdiction, such as a town, county, township, borough, or parish.

tax collector A local-level government employee responsible for the distribution of tax bills to property owners within his taxing jurisdiction and the collection of the tax. This function may be carried out by the town clerk, and is usually not done by the tax assessor.

tax rate A rate applied to the assessed value of your property to determine the amount of property tax to be paid. It is calculated by dividing the budget (the total of the monies to be spent in three ways: bonded indebtedness, schools, and all other services) of a taxing municipality, less any anticipated revenues from non-property-tax sources, by the total assessed value of the assessment roll (all taxable properties). An individual value (assessed value) is multiplied by the rate to obtain an individual tax. The tax rate can be expressed in dollars per $100 or $1,000 of assessed value or in millage (thousandths of a dollar).

Index